AMERICAN CARS
of the 1950s

First published in 2008 by Motorbooks, an imprint of MBI Publishing Company LLC, Galtier Plaza, Suite 200, 380 Jackson Street, St. Paul, MN 55101 USA

Motorbooks titles are also available at discounts in bulk quantity for industrial or sales-promotional use. For details write to Special Sales Manager at MBI Publishing Company, Galtier Plaza, Suite 200, 380 Jackson Street, St. Paul, MN 55101 USA.

To find out more about our books, join us online at www.motorbooks.com.

About the authors: Robert Genat is an accomplished author and photographer who has written over 25 books for MBI Publishing Company, including a number of Mopar muscle car histories. He and his wife, Robin, own and operate Zone Five Photo. He lives in Encinitas, California.

An acclaimed photographer and author, David Newhardt's work includes writing and photography for books such as *Mustang: 1964¹/₂–1973* and *Firebird Trans Am*, photography for *Mopar Muscle: Fifty Years*, and many more titles. He lives with his wife in Pasadena, California.

Frontis: With twenty-five vertical bars, the Skylark's grille takes patience to clean.

Front cover: Hooded headlights were a stylistic element that Ford employed across most of its lineup, including the 1957 Thunderbird.

Back cover: *(Left)* Quad headlights debuted in 1958 in an effort to modernize the Bonneville's appearance.

(Middle) With a Hemi under the hood, full instrumentation helped monitor the engine's vitals.

(Right) As befitting an American car with sporting pretensions, the Nash Healey wore wire wheel hubcaps emblazoned with the Nash emblem.

Library of Congress Cataloging-in-Publication Data

Genat, Robert, 1945–
    American cars of the 1950s / Robert Genat ; photography by David Newhardt.
        p. cm.
    ISBN: 978-0-7603-3230-6 (softbound)
        1. Automobiles—United States—History.
        2. Automobiles—United States—Pictorial works.
        3. Automobiles—Collectors and collecting—United States.   I. Title.
    TL23.G448 2007
    629.2220973'09045--dc22

                                                            2007025879

Editor: Peter Schletty
Designer: Brenda C. Canales

Printed in China

Contents

Introduction

The decade of the 1950s in America was unlike any other. Those who document pop culture look to the 1950s for hundreds of iconic images, from hula-hoops to *I Love Lucy* to the powerful chrome-clad automobiles we all love.

In the 1950s, America's industrial base was fully geared for consumer products after several years of developing and producing war goods. The American public was poised, cash in hand, with greater buying power than ever before. This prosperity led to a suburban housing boom. With the GI Bill, the government enabled thousands of veterans to attend college and buy their first homes. These new homes would be filled with blenders, mixers, clock radios, and televisions—appliances to make life easier and more enjoyable.

The new housing tracts were built out in the suburbs, miles away from the city. This required the purchase of a car to get to work and to go shopping downtown. What you drove became as important as where you lived. Any new car in a neighborhood driveway would soon become the focus of interested neighbors. The proud owner of the new car would gladly show the local men the spiffy new interior and lift the hood to explain to them why he had bought a better and more powerful engine. The wives would come out to view the new car and comment on the attractive two-tone color scheme and bright, chrome-clad bumpers.

In the 1950s, families were intensely loyal to a manufacturer or to a brand of car. There were Chevrolet, Ford, and Plymouth families. Very rarely would someone who always bought GM products change over to a Ford or Chrysler product. One would move up in class of car but would not switch brands. Each of the Big Three automobile companies developed several lines of cars to fit every rung in the social ladder. At General Motors, Chevrolet was the entry car. The steps up in General Motors models included Pontiac, Oldsmobile, Buick, and then finally, a Cadillac. Ford Motor Company had its own pecking order that included Ford, Mercury, and then Lincoln. Someone loyal to Chrysler products started with a Plymouth, then graduated to a Dodge, a DeSoto, and, for luxury, upgraded to a Chrysler or Chrysler Imperial. With each succeeding model there was more chrome, more power, and upgraded interiors. And then there were those independent thinkers who opted for a Nash or Studebaker.

Sports cars, long popular in Europe, started to appear on American streets in the 1950s. While overseas during the war, American GIs had been exposed to these trendy cars and found them fun to drive. Many brought them back after the war or had them imported. The American car companies were quick to notice this developing trend, and in 1953 Chevrolet debuted a two-seat sports car: the Corvette. In 1955, Ford released its two-seat Thunderbird sports car. Both of these cars are firmly imbedded in the culture and the imagery of the 1950s.

The 1950s also saw the first shots fired in the horsepower war. Ford had long held the torch for V-8 power with its flathead engine, but in 1949 both Oldsmobile and Cadillac offered new overhead-valve V-8 engines. In 1955, Chevrolet released its new 265-cubic-inch V-8, and the world of automotive engines would never be the same. The new engine offered a compact size, extreme horsepower potential, and exceptional fuel efficiency. Soon, almost every make and model offered a V-8 engine. The ads for each brand of 1950s car touted its unique and powerful V-8 engine. Oldsmobile's advertising copywriters developed the "Rocket" theme for its line of V-8 engines, which blended perfectly with America's new interest in space. Other manufacturers also jumped on the engine brand name bandwagon, giving us Pontiac's Strato-Streak V-8, Chrysler's FirePower V-8, and Chevrolet's "Turbo-Fire" V-8. By the end of the decade, Detroit's automakers were offering engines with amazing amounts of power.

Within a few years, these engines would be powering a new generation of muscle cars.

One big boon to the automobile industry in the 1950s was the National Interstate and Defense Highways Act. Enacted on June 29, 1956, this legislation created the nation's largest public works project, designating $25 billion over a ten-year period for new interstate highways. Much of the money came from increased taxes on gasoline, tires, and cars. One of the incentives for then-president Dwight Eisenhower to sign the bill was the way a national highway system would allow the government to easily move troops and materials in time of war. For the automobile owner, this new interstate highway system meant greatly reduced travel times between cities. And with the new V-8-powered cars traveling at high speeds on these highways, the trip would be much easier and more enjoyable.

With this new system of roads, Americans were now using the automobile for extended trips. A coast-to-coast trip could be accomplished in a matter of days rather than weeks. To facilitate these longer drives, the auto manufacturers added luxury options like signal-seeking radios, power seats, power windows, and air conditioning. Seats were trimmed in fine brocade cloth or soft leather.

In addition to horsepower, the cars of the 1950s will long be remembered for their dramatic styling. The tail fin that started as an homage to the jet aircraft soon became a caricature of itself. The fin grew larger and more dramatic with each new model. Accenting those fins were two- and three-tone paint schemes and lots of chrome. Americans will long remember these spectacular cars with great affection.

General Motors

General Motors

General Motors became a powerful automobile manufacturer in the 1950s by combining advanced V-8 technology with elegant and often extravagant Harley Earl designs. GM had the foresight to produce the right mix of cars to quench America's thirst for transportation. Each of GM's car lines produced a specific vehicle that appealed to a different market segment. The car lines were also structured for upwardly mobile consumers who started with a Chevy and ended with a Cadillac—America's standard for excellence in the 1950s. A test for the impact of General Motors' cars of the 1950s is the number of iconic automotive images their cars have created. The image of a Cadillac tail fin is as recognizable worldwide as the hula-hoop or Lucy Ricardo.

Chevrolet

Chevrolet entered the 1950s with simple transportation cars that were redesigned for 1949. One change that came about for the 1950s models was the addition of the Bel Air—America's first low-cost hardtop. This was Chevrolet's first step up the ladder of automotive honor. Because car models come and go, Chevrolet's product planners may have had no idea of how popular the Bel Air nameplate would become in the future.

Previous spread: 1956 Bel Air Sedan

Chevy first introduced the Bel Air and its entire line of cars in 1949 and continued to build them through 1952. In 1953, Chevrolet introduced its freshly restyled cars that looked boxy compared to the full-size Ford that was on the market a year earlier. But Chevrolet was able to outsell the Ford by a small margin. The job became harder in 1954, when Ford released its new overhead V-8 and squeaked out a small edge in sales. But all that would end in 1955.

Most products in the automotive world are *e*volutionary, building each year on past improvements. But the small-block, 265-cubic-inch engine that Chevrolet introduced in 1955 was *re*volutionary. Chevrolet's engineers created an engine that was lightweight, powerful, fuel efficient, and well engineered. It also had great potential for horsepower. In addition, Chevrolet designed a great car around that engine. The new Chevrolet had subtle fins and headlights like the intakes on a jet fighter. Designers did away with the massive toothy grille and opted for a much more upscale egg crate design that would be seen on Chevys during the rest of the decade. Chevrolet's product planners felt that with the rush to the suburbs in the 1950s, car buyers might like an upscale station wagon. To fulfill this expected market need they created the Nomad, a classy two-door station wagon. The American public loved the new Chevrolets.

Chevrolet's 1956 models disappointed no one. The addition of Zora Arkus-Duntov to the engineering team led to the installation of a dual-quad, 225-horsepower engine. A light facelift gave the car more character, and sales remained high.

With the 1957 Chevy, Chevrolet's design team created what would eventually be an icon of the 1950s. It had the look of a jet fighter with bold tail fins and headlight bezels. Chevrolet's engineers added an egg-crate anodized aluminum grille to the '57 model. The Bel Air's grille was anodized in gold. They also added anodized aluminum to the Bel Air's quarter panel. This would be Chevrolet's first use of anodized aluminum, which added visual interest because of its texture and color. It was also inexpensive to manufacture.

Chevrolet's engine team tweaked the 1957 Chevrolet by increasing the displacement of the small block from 265 to 283 cubic inches. This small addition in displacement made a big difference in performance. The 283 could be selected with horsepower ratings from 185 with a two-barrel carburetor to 283 on the fuel-injected engine.

As good as the 1957 Chevrolet looked and with the wide variety of powertrain options available, it still did not beat Ford in sales. This would also be the last year for the attractive Nomad wagon.

In 1958, Chevrolet designed an all-new car that looked more like a Cadillac than did its 1957 predecessor. Chevrolet designed its '58 model to be longer, lower, and wider than any previous Chevy. The engine group contributed with the addition of a 348-cubic-inch engine with a base horsepower rating of 250 and optional 315 horsepower. In 1958, the Impala replaced the Bel Air as the top-of-the-line model. It could only be purchased as a two-door hardtop or convertible. Chevrolet retained the Bel Air model, but it had much less content than the Impala.

For 1959, instead of simply revamping the 1958 model, Chevrolet did the unusual by completely redesigning the entire vehicle. A "one-year" car (in this case the 1958 model) is unusual in the automotive world. In order to amortize costs, a manufacturer will typically face-lift a model for a second (and often a third) year of production. Chevrolet created an unusual design with bat-type fins and teardrop-shaped taillights. The Impala again reigned supreme, but this time Chevrolet added a four-door hardtop to the list of models. Horsepower options also expanded with the top engine now rated at 335.

In the 1950s, the Chevrolet went from a plain Jane passenger car to a glamorous Hollywood starlet. Along the way, the engine group set the stage for the upcoming muscle car era by developing two different, but powerful, V-8 engines.

Pontiac

General Motors positioned the Pontiac as the next step up from a Chevrolet. The late 1940s and early 1950s Pontiacs, while built on a Chevy chassis, offered more power and standard features than a Chevrolet. In 1950 Pontiac introduced the Catalina, its first true hardtop and convertible model. The Pontiac was redesigned for 1953 and 1954. The 1955 Pontiac boasted more than 100 new or revised features, the most important of which was the new 287-cubic-inch V-8 engine. Pontiac also offered an upscale station wagon named the Safari—its version of Chevrolet's Nomad.

In 1956, Semon "Bunkie" Knudsen became the general manager of Pontiac. He enjoyed high-performance cars and immediately set out to change Pontiac's image. For 1957, he got rid of the chrome hood stripes and added performance. With the limited time Knudsen had before the release of the 1957 models, he created the Bonneville as a high-performance image car for Pontiac. In 1958, with the completely restyled Pontiac, he also included a Bonneville.

Pontiac, like Chevrolet in 1959, came out with an entirely new car. These were the first Pontiacs over which Knudsen had complete control, and they were amazing. This was also the first year to feature a split grille, a Pontiac design tradition that continues to this day. Pontiac engineers also created the smooth riding "Wide-Track" chassis by moving the wheels slightly outboard. Knudsen increased the displacement of the

V-8 engine to 389 and offered it in several performance versions, including one that developed 345 horsepower.

The 1950s saw a major change in Pontiac. The car went from a sedate sedan that could be driven by a spinster librarian to a Bonneville convertible with 345 horsepower. Pontiac's performance image would continue to grow through the 1960s as well.

Buick

During the 1950s, the Buick was generally considered an upscale, establishment vehicle, one that might be driven by a professional person, such as a banker.

Buick entered the 1950s with massive grilles, distinctive portholes, and slashing side moldings that dominated its styling. In 1953, Buick introduced its first 322-cubic-inch V-8, power steering, and a 12-volt electrical system. The new V-8 was burdened by the automatic transmission that Buick's engineers had created—the Dynaflow. While smooth during shifting, the Dynaflow detracted from the performance of the new V-8 and soon became the butt of many jokes.

The 1955–1957 Buicks were exceptionally well designed and attractive. In 1955, Buick had a banner year, selling over three quarters of a million cars. Buick also introduced its first four-door hardtop in 1955. Like much of the American public, Buick's design team was fascinated with the aviation world and did an excellent job of adding highly integrated fins onto its cars during the 1950s. The engine group did its best to provide more horsepower each year, with the 1957 engines rated at 250 and 300 horsepower.

The 1958 Buicks did not meet the high design standards of earlier models. They looked fatter and as if the factory had come across a bin of extra chrome moldings and wanted to add as many as possible to each car. While sales were down for all carmakers in 1958, Buick fared much worse by selling fewer than 250,000 cars—well below the sales record set in 1955.

The 1959 Buick was a far cry from its 1958 predecessor. It did feature a massive grille and an almost "frowning" front end with angled headlights, but the sides were clean and swept rearward into tastefully canted fins. Buick's product planners also dropped two decades worth of model names and created new ones. The Special was now the LeSabre, Invicta replaced Century, the Super became the Electra, and the Roadmaster was now the Electra 225 (or "deuce and a quarter" as its was commonly called). Buick also offered a 401-cubic-inch engine rated at 325 horsepower.

In 1959, Buick unknowingly positioned itself for the coming few years by having the small German Opel on its showroom floors. In 1960, the American buying public wanted small cars, and Buick was ready with the Opel. Opel was a GM subsidiary, and Buick had been selected as the domestic outlet for this vehicle.

Oldsmobile

Oldsmobile entered the 1950s as if it had been shot out of a cannon. It offered some of the best styling of any American car, a new overhead-valve V-8 engine, and a well-proven automatic transmission, which few cars on the road had at that time.

Oldsmobile's impressive new V-8 displaced 303 cubic inches and developed 135 horsepower. Olds would use this engine through the 1953 model year. It worked exceptionally well with the Hydra-Matic automatic transmission that GM's engineers had developed. NASCAR racers soon found that the new Old's V-8 was well suited for racing, and Oldsmobiles set many records in the late 1940s and early 1950s.

Olds designers did a wonderful job of restyling the 1954 Oldsmobile. Features included a wraparound windshield and wraparound back window. They also added a notched side molding that facilitated the then-trendy two-tone paint schemes. The 1955 models received a light facelift and won the hearts of Americans. Customers bought Oldsmobiles in record numbers, pushing Olds up to number four in overall sales. The 1956 models also did well in sales, although Plymouth passed Olds for that fourth spot on the sales sheet.

Oldsmobile designers did a masterful job of styling the 1957 Olds. They shunned the idea of flamboyant fins in favor of a much more tasteful design that incorporated a *Jetsons* rocket ship look. The 1957 Olds two-door hardtop offered a design featuring a slick, three-piece rear window treatment that included longitudinal beads on the roof. Olds continued to be a 1950s performance leader by offering its famous J-2 tri-power carburetors as an option on the 1957 models.

In the midst of an economic recession in 1958, Olds did exceptionally well. The design staff gave in to the trends and added modest fins and lots of chrome. Even with a reduction in overall sales, Olds regained the fourth spot on the sales leader board with its 1958 offerings.

Like other 1959 General Motors models, the design of the '59 Olds went from the understated to the ridiculous. The small oval taillights with integral fins extended upward from the beltline to a level above the deck lid. The new Oldsmobile also got wider, longer, and heavier. But, the 1959 Olds sold well, maintaining the division's fifth place ranking.

General Motors' Olds division did exceptionally well during the 1950s. It led the way with a well-designed and powerful V-8 engine and outstanding styling.

Cadillac

General Motors had been working since the 1920s to position the Cadillac as America's premier luxury car. As the 1950s dawned, GM's years of hard work were about to pay off. The excellent design work on its modestly finned 1948 models and on the new overhead valve V-8 engine released in 1949 set the stage for an exciting decade for the Cadillac.

Cadillac entered the 1950s with a powerful V-8 engine and a true two-door hardtop, features that Packard, Lincoln, or Chrysler could not claim. Cadillac engineers also added a superb suspension that provided an excellent ride and the smooth shifting Hydra-Matic automatic transmission.

The 1950 through 1953 Cadillacs were similar-looking with a massive front bumper and grille and simulated air scoop quarter panels with small tail fins in the rear. In 1952, Cadillac designers added what they called "poke" to the car with the addition of "Dagmar"-style front bumper bullets. These distinctive bullets would be seen on the front of Cadillacs for the next five years.

In 1954 Cadillac rolled out a new and much bigger car. Cadillac designers lengthened and widened the latest version while adding more poke to the front end. They added power steering as a standard item and retained the iconic Cadillac tail fins. Cadillac's engineering team was able to pull 230 horsepower out of the V-8 engine. The 1955 and 1956 models were facelifts of the outstanding 1954 design. Throughout these years Cadillac's sales were exceptionally strong. Cadillac sold three cars for every Lincoln sold in 1956.

Cadillac's engineers found even more horse-power in 1957, and the designers did another masterful job of restyling America's favorite luxury car. In the 1950s, Cadillac's design team knew how to preserve the "Cadillac look" with each successive body change. Every year they designed the massive grille and signature fins. People on the street knew when a Caddy was coming toward them or going away from them. In 1957 these fins got larger and the taillights moved down to a position just above the rear bumper—but it was unmistakably a Cadillac.

The fins on the 1958 Cadillac grew larger and more defined. But sales lagged a bit, and the blame was shared between the economy and the fact that GM added too much chrome to the car.

In 1959, Cadillac introduced a car that would go down in history for its outlandish fins and audacious graphics. It's as if designers had lost all sense of Cadillac's style and place in history. They created something over the top in an attempt to outdo the competition. The new Cadillac was also big and expensive; the weight of the lightest 1959 Cadillac was 4,600 pounds with a base price of over $1.00 per pound. But the Cadillac's kitschy fins made their mark and have become an enduring icon of the 1950s and a symbol of the excesses of the auto industry in the late 1950s.

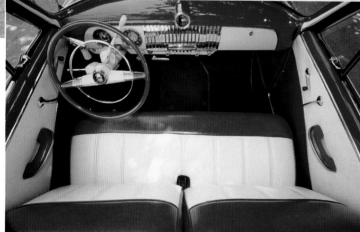

Spacious was the word in 1952 when the Bel Air beckoned drivers and passengers alike.

(above) Chevrolet introduced a new grille for 1952, yet the core Chevy "value for the money" still ruled the lineup.

In 1952, American forces were fighting in the Korean conflict. The government put itself first in line for natural resources to build weapons of war. This created material shortages that hurt production of all American automobiles.

(above) Flowing lines hinted at aerodynamic design, while tasteful chrome accents tickled the eye.

The Chevrolet Bow Tie emblem cut the wind on the prow of the 1952 Bel Air. The huge, heavy hood was built of solid steel and was a chore to lift.

(above) The Roadmaster was a beautifully proportioned sedan that came equipped with a new V-8, celebrating Buick's 50th anniversary.

Buick built 79,237 Roadmasters in model year 1953, and one of the reasons for that success was Buick's high profile on the latest invention to invade American homes, the television. The Roadmaster was built on a 121.5-inch wheelbase, and the relatively light weight combined with the robust V-8 gave credence to Buick's claim that it was the "Star of the silky way."

"Venti-Ports" have been a Buick tradition for decades, with four on each side of the voluptuous front fenders denoting an eight-cylinder engine.

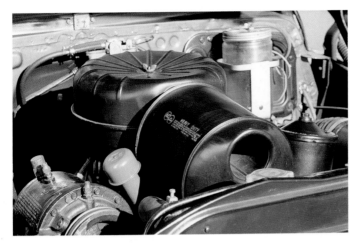

Beneath the large air cleaner was a 332-cubic-inch Fireball V-8 developing 188 horsepower by using a Carter WCFB-996S four-barrel carburetor. Buick boasted that it had vertical valves and a 12-volt electrical system.

Standard power steering made maneuvering the large car child's play. Per the custom of the time, the steering wheel was large and close to the driver.

(above) Costing a whopping $5,000, the Skylark was built one-car-per-dealer, for a total production of just 1,690 units.

(inset) Billed as a "six-passenger sports car," the Skylark had plenty of room for lucky passengers.

Due to the lofty price, many Skylarks simply sat on showroom floors, pulling in potential buyers. Buick fitted the Skylark with virtually every option in the book, including a V-8 engine, power steering, brakes, and windows.

(above) With its lowered convertible top and 40-spoke Kelsey-Hayes wire wheels, the Skylark looked like something from a customizer, not a factory.

With twenty-five vertical bars, the Skylark's grille took patience to clean.

(above) Its fiberglass body was only 51 inches high, and a Cadillac V-8 generating 250 horse-power, powered it.

Unlike the front of the car, the Cadillac Le Mans wore thin, graceful tail fins with a minimum of brightwork.

Four Cadillac Le Mans were built in 1953, and styling elements from these vehicles showed up on production Cadillacs for years to come. The La Mans had a single bench seat designed to hold up to three people, and its convertible top had a feature that automatically raised the top when a moisture sensor detected rain. GM justified the building of this rolling eye candy, advertising that "by finding out which features you, the public, like best in these far-in-advance models, we can set our sights on the long task of including them on production cars."

Replicating the look of a turbine, the wheels of the Cadillac Le Mans were cast aluminum.

As was the practice, lavish use of chrome gave the Cadillac an imposing presence.

Chevrolet created a legend when it developed the 265-cubic-inch V-8 engine. In 1955, oil filters were optional, and those customers who did not order one saw shorter engine life. The canister for this oil filter mounted on top of the intake manifold.

(above) Chevrolet hit one out of the park with the release of the 1955 Bel Air model, its modern design breaking the staid postwar styling mold.

Slender roof pillars helped impart a sporty image, as well as aided in minimizing blind spots.

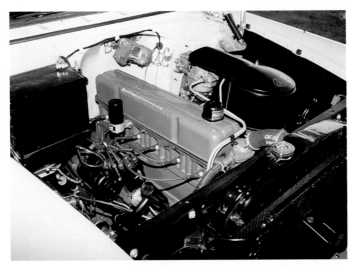

Base One-Fifty models started at $1,593 with a six-cylinder engine.

With a new-for-1955 V-8 under the hood, the long needle on the speedometer would sweep across the face with vigor.

(above) The 1955 Bel Air rode on 6.70 x 15-inch tubeless tires. Front tread measured 58 inches, while the rear tread came in at 58.8 inches.

The Chevrolet crest and Bel Air script adorned each side of the 1955 model. Gentle kick-up of the belt-line broke the full-length span of sheet metal.

In 1955, American car buyers came out in full force to buy a total of 7.1 million cars, 1.7 of which were built by Chevrolet. The most impressive statistic was that Chevrolet owned 44 percent of the low-price market. Because of its excellent styling and performance, the 1955 Chevrolet quickly picked up the nickname, "The Hot One."

Nothing said speed like a stylized jet on the hood of your car. With a hood as heavy as the 1955 Bel Air's, the hood ornament was a handy grab handle.

Hooded headlights were a styling touch that Chevrolet, as well as the rest of Detroit, embraced in 1955.

(above) The Del Ray coupe was a member of the middle-priced Two-Ten family of the 1955 Chevrolet lineup.

Airy, comfortable, and stylish, the 1955 Del Ray interior used twin "fans" as stylistic elements. The left fan held the speedometer, while the right side contained a radio speaker.

As the entry-level model in the popular 210-Series, the Del Ray enjoyed upgraded interior appointments and exterior brightwork to differentiate it from the base 150-Series.

Displacing 265 cubic inches and rated at 170 horsepower with the Powerglide transmission, the Chevrolet V-8 gave birth to a long line of successful engines that continues to the present day.

For 1955, Chevrolet fitted a wrap-around taillight to the Del Ray, replacing it in 1956 with a "bullet" lens.

The Nomad was released as a mid-year model, thus helping to keep sales low. Only 6,103 were built in 1955. Ribs on the roof panel prevented "oil-canning," the vibration incurred by velocity and vehicle harmonics.

(above) The Nomad was only available in the Bel Air line, and as such was at the upper end of the pricing scale, starting at $2,571.

Two-tone seat covers, plush carpeting, and headliner trim set the Nomad apart from the more austere 150-Series Chevrolets.

Rear seat access was a challenge, but the Nomad had perfect proportions.

The small "V" beneath the Nomad's taillight indicated that a V-8 lived under the hood.

(above) An absence of exterior trim in the rear quarters gave the Nomad a clean, uncluttered appearance. The egg-crate grille was inspired by Ferrari.

When Chevrolet designer Carl Renner's two-door wagon concept debuted in 1954 on the Corvette Nomad shown at the Waldorf Astoria Hotel in New York City, it caused a huge response. While the Corvette never saw a production wagon, the idea translated well into the Bel Air line.

Unlike modern vehicles, the 1955 Nomad's engine compartment was home to the 265-cubic-inch V-8 and little else.

Chevrolet used a classy gold-tone badge on the tailgate of the 1955 Nomad.

The standard two-tone exterior treatment was carried into the interior, as seats and door panels wore contrasting material.

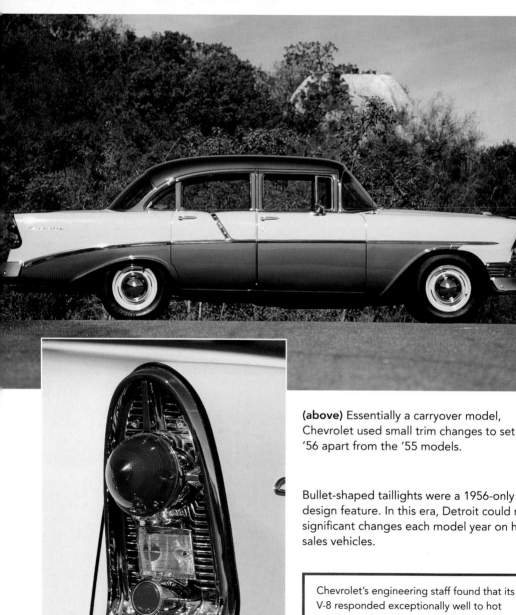

(above) Essentially a carryover model, Chevrolet used small trim changes to set the '56 apart from the '55 models.

Bullet-shaped taillights were a 1956-only design feature. In this era, Detroit could make significant changes each model year on high-sales vehicles.

Chevrolet's engineering staff found that its new V-8 responded exceptionally well to hot rodding add-ons like dual-quad carburetors and hot camshafts. The first of Chevrolet's hot engines was the optional 225-horsepower V-8 offered in 1956.

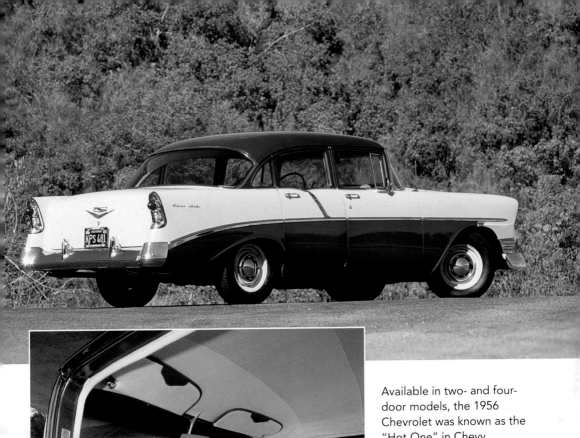

Available in two- and four-door models, the 1956 Chevrolet was known as the "Hot One" in Chevy advertisements.

Three adults could fit comfortably on the roomy front bench seat. Passengers in the rear enjoyed similar accommodations.

(above) Chevrolet stunned the automotive world in 1955 with the debut of the Bel Air hardtop, an inviting mixture of style, performance, and affordability. This blend continued into 1956.

Detroit embraced the tail fin in the 1950s, as an homage to the Jet Age that was revolutionizing America.

Chevrolet capitalized on America's desire for a sleek, moderately priced car that broke the pre-war styling mold. The two-door sedan sold in the neighborhood of $2,100, a solid value.

All new sheet metal and a soon-to-be legendary V-8 allowed Chevrolet to sell 104,849 two-door sedan Bel Airs in 1956.

Tasteful restrained styling grabbed the public's attention in 1956, and continues to appeal to people today.

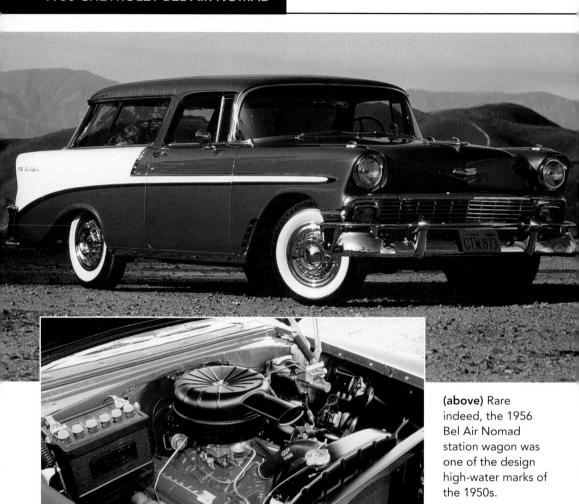

(above) Rare indeed, the 1956 Bel Air Nomad station wagon was one of the design high-water marks of the 1950s.

With 265 cubic inches under the hood, the 1956 Nomad could take advantage of the burgeoning Interstate Highway System.

Base prices for 1956 Chevrolets:
Six-cylinder-equipped 150 sedan: $1,665
V-8-equipped Bel Air hardtop: $2,082
V-8-equipped Bel Air convertible: $2,237
V-8-equipped Nomad: $2,482

Perfect proportions helped create a stylistic classic. With the huge, rear side glass, blind spots were virtually non-existent.

In order to maintain the sleek lines, the stylists hid the fuel filler behind the driver-side taillight.

(**above**) The costliest Bel Air in 1956 was the convertible model, starting at $2,443.

The runaway sales success of the 1955–1956 Chevrolets lifted Chevrolet chief engineer Ed Cole to general manager. A hard-core car guy, he felt that performance would sell a car as well as style. Cole brought famed engineer Zora Arkus-Duntov into the Chevrolet fold, clearing the way for the introduction of fuel injection and multiple racing victories.

Chevrolet mounted the glove box beneath the radio. On the face of the radio were CONELRAD National Defense System emblems, noting where listeners would tune to in case of an emergency.

(above) A full-length chrome spear was unique to the 1956 Bel Air, giving it a touch more visual flash than the base models.

Seating for six was standard in most 1950s-era American vehicles, and the 1956 Bel Air convertible was no exception. A roomy trunk made family vacations a snap.

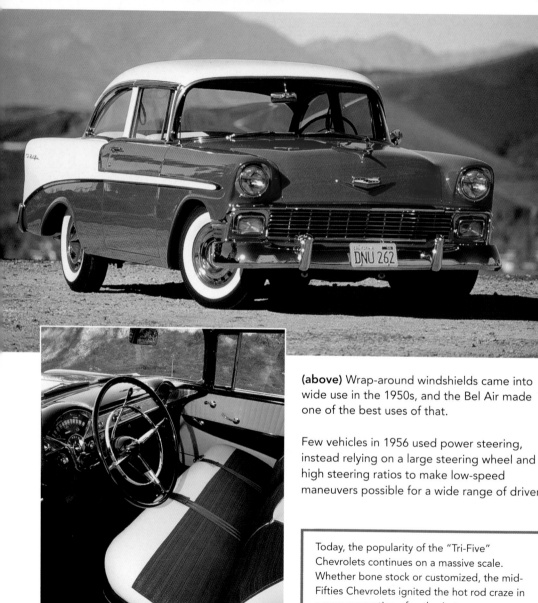

(above) Wrap-around windshields came into wide use in the 1950s, and the Bel Air made one of the best uses of that.

Few vehicles in 1956 used power steering, instead relying on a large steering wheel and high steering ratios to make low-speed maneuvers possible for a wide range of drivers.

Today, the popularity of the "Tri-Five" Chevrolets continues on a massive scale. Whether bone stock or customized, the mid-Fifties Chevrolets ignited the hot rod craze in a new generation of enthusiasts.

(above) Thin roof pillars contributed to a sleek greenhouse, as well as virtually eliminating blind spots.

Depending on the depth of a buyer's pocketbook, the Bel Air could be equipped with a V-8 ranging from 170 horsepower to 225 horsepower, sourced from the Corvette. The V-8 weighed 40 pounds less than Chevrolet's own six-cylinder engine.

(above) Buick was proud of the fact that the 1957 models were lower than preceding years. Venti-Ports on the front fenders denoted that a V-8 lived under the hood.

In the 1950s, each of General Motors' divisions developed its own V-8 engine. GM was flush with cash, allowing this extravagance. But GM also used it as a marketing ploy to sell the exclusivity of each brand. Those loyal to Buick loved the Buick V-8 and would brag to other car owners about its power and reliability. The engine in this 1957 Buick was rated at 300 horsepower.

Detroit embraced the glory of heavy chrome, and the 1957 Buick was one of the banner vehicles. Solid, heavy bumpers were functional, keeping the lush bodywork intact.

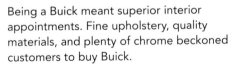

Being a Buick meant superior interior appointments. Fine upholstery, quality materials, and plenty of chrome beckoned customers to buy Buick.

Jet-Age fins bestowed power and strength, at least visually, to Detroit's 1957 offerings. Buick used a 364-cubic-inch V-8 to get the hefty vehicle underway.

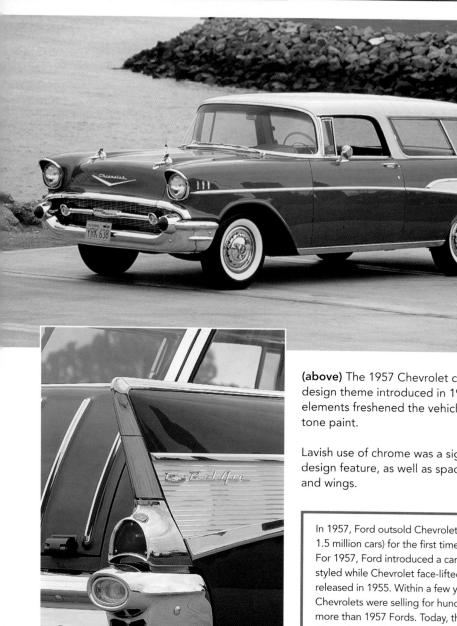

(above) The 1957 Chevrolet continued the design theme introduced in 1955, but stylistic elements freshened the vehicle, including tri-tone paint.

Lavish use of chrome was a signature late-50s design feature, as well as space-age fins and wings.

In 1957, Ford outsold Chevrolet (1.6 million to 1.5 million cars) for the first time in many years. For 1957, Ford introduced a car that was freshly styled while Chevrolet face-lifted the car it first released in 1955. Within a few years, used 1957 Chevrolets were selling for hundreds of dollars more than 1957 Fords. Today, the 1957 Chevrolet's tailfin has become an iconic image of the 1950s, and the car commands a premium price among collectors.

Chevrolet entered the age of the fins in 1957, in an effort to bring the space age to Earth.

Hooded headlights and Dagmar bumper guards were two of the design features that characterized the latter half of 1950s styling.

(above) With twin "rockets" on the hood, the 1957 Chevrolet embraced the look of high-performance aircraft, no small thing as America was poised to enter the space race.

In the 1950s, Detroit felt that if *some* chrome and brightwork was good, *more* was even better. The radio and surrounding panel in the 1957 Chevy were proof of this line of thinking.

In 1957, Chevrolet would be the first of the GM divisions to make extensive use of anodized aluminum exterior trim. Chevy's designers used it for the egg-crate grille in all models, and quarter trim and V-8 "V" trunk and hood emblems on the Bel Airs. Anodized aluminum provided a low-cost alternative to chrome plating.

By using a dip in the shoulder line, Chevrolet stylists injected interest into what could have been a long, boring line of sheet metal.

With two, four-barrel carburetors atop the 283-cubic-inch V-8, the 1957 Chevrolet boasted 245 horsepower, more than enough to sprint ahead in stoplight encounters.

(above) For the buyer who wanted to work on a tan as well as breathe fresh air, the 1957 Chevrolet convertible was one of the most stylish ways to enjoy Mother Nature.

Boasting one horsepower per cubic inch, Rochester fuel injection made its debut in 1957 in both the 1957 Chevrolet and the Corvette.

In 1957, Chevrolet released its Rochester fuel injection unit as an option on both the Corvette and its passenger cars with horsepower ratings of 250 and 283. The 283-horsepower engine could only be ordered with a manual transmission, but the 250-horsepower engine could be ordered with an automatic or manual transmission. Chevrolet would continue to offer fuel injection in its passenger cars through 1959 and on Corvettes through 1965.

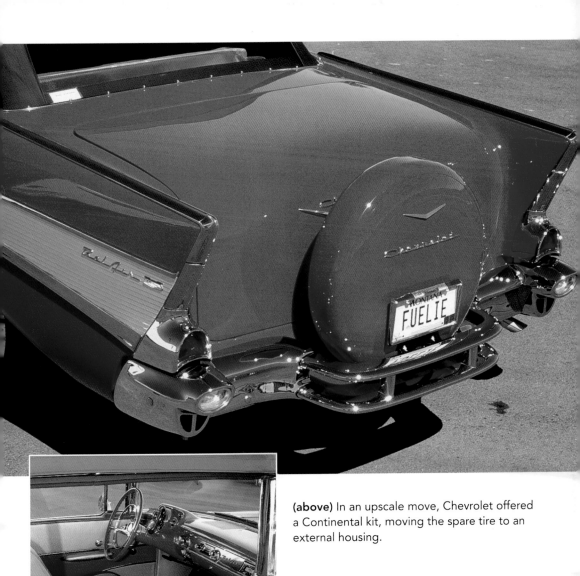

(above) In an upscale move, Chevrolet offered a Continental kit, moving the spare tire to an external housing.

With rich, two-tone upholstery and a big bench seat, the whole family got to go for a ride.

(above) In 1957, one only had to look to the Bel Air to see that Chevrolet was serious about having fun. America embraced the crisp lines and sporty look.

For many years, Chevrolet offered the durable two-speed Powerglide automatic transmission.

Prices for a new 1957 Chevrolet with the base 185-horsepower V-8 engine:
150 two-door sedan: $1,902
Bel Air hardtop: $2,183
Bel Air convertible: $2,380
Nomad: $2,609
Corvette: $3,176

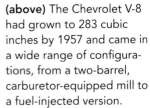

(above) The Chevrolet V-8 had grown to 283 cubic inches by 1957 and came in a wide range of configurations, from a two-barrel, carburetor-equipped mill to a fuel-injected version.

The '57 Bel Air mirrored America, exuding optimism and thinking big. Chevrolet sold more than 1.5 million vehicles in 1957.

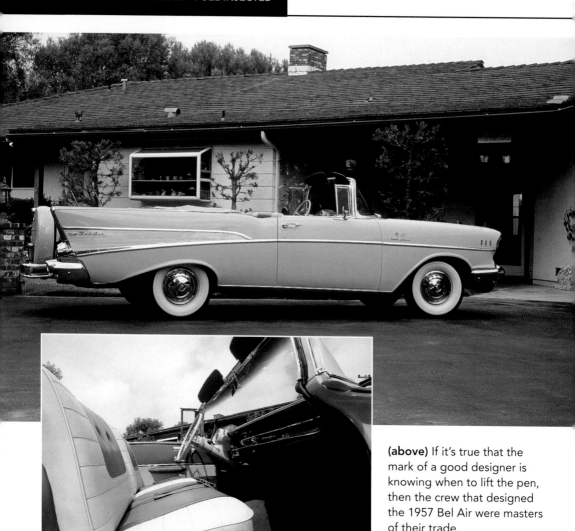

(above) If it's true that the mark of a good designer is knowing when to lift the pen, then the crew that designed the 1957 Bel Air were masters of their trade.

Chevrolet prided itself on providing good value for the money, and that included a comfortable and stylish interior. Fierce cornering was not encouraged, as the occupants would slide from side to side.

With its crisp lines, sprightly performance, and moderate price, it surprised few that the 1957 Bel Air was a sales success. The up-market Bel Air was loaded with subtle touches to set it apart from "regular" Chevrolets, such as gold-tone badging, two-tone interiors, and special brightwork.

(above) This was the first year for a fuel-injected engine to be fitted to a Chevrolet, and the Bel Air shared this potent powerplant with the Corvette.

Chevrolet used these fins for just one year, 1957; little did anyone know they would become a cultural icon.

Chevrolet treated the Bel Air to a mild re-design for 1957, including bumper "bombs" and a bar that stretched across the grille.

While the two-door Bel Air was the first pick for the style-conscious, the four-door was what most people put into the garage. This model sold an impressive 254,331 units, putting it on top of all the Bel Air variants in vehicles sold.

Though the 1957 Bel Air rode on the same 115-inch wheelbase as the previous two years' models, the '57 used increasingly large fins to "stretch" the look of the top-line model, as well as adding 2.5 inches to the overall length.

Dramatic tail fins were used only one year, resulting in an instant classic. Chevrolet designers used arcing side trim to give relief to the slab sides.

Two-tone finishes were standard with the Bel Air, creating instant drama. Chevrolet moved its Bow Tie to the grille cross-bar.

For the first time, Chevrolet used an anodized mesh grille on its V-8 models in 1957. This was the first year that, according to Chevrolet's advertising, a passenger car used an engine that produced one horsepower per cubic inch of displacement.

Chevrolet priced the two-door sedan at $2,238. But with an option list as long as your arm, it could raise the final price to considerably more.

The small-block Chevrolet V-8, which debuted in 1955, carries forward to the present day. Lightweight, strong, and easy to hop up, it is arguably the most popular automotive engine in history.

(above) In an effort to modernize the vehicle, Chevrolet lowered the car 1.5 inches and lengthened it 2.5 inches from the 1956 model.

While Detroit was building vehicles with ever more horsepower, Washington D. C. cracked down on what they perceived as a horsepower war between the manufacturers. General Motors publicly embraced a ban on supporting motorsports, yet the performance lived on.

The thin chrome circle within the steering wheel was depressed to sound the horn. With a fuel-injected engine sourced from the Corvette, it wasn't difficult to swing the speedometer needle into the upper portion of the dial.

(above) Lifted from the 1957 Corvette, the mechanically fuel-injected 283-cubic-inch V-8 used both hydraulic lifters (250 horsepower at 5,000 rpm) and solid lifters (283 horsepower at 6,200 rpm).

The optional Continental Tire Kit mounted the spare on the rear bumper, but access to the huge trunk was compromised.

(above) This was to be the last year for the storied two-door Nomad, a station wagon with sharp styling and flawless proportions. Unfortunately, poor sales doomed it.

Chevrolet built the two-door Nomad for only three years. Only 6,103 Nomads were built in 1957. Starting in 1958, Chevy put the Nomad name on a full-sized four-door station wagon that wore Impala trim.

As the Nomad was based only on the up-market Bel Air, it came very comfortably equipped, inside and out.

Hubcaps fitted with tri-bar spinners were meant to evoke knock-off wheels.

Vertical ribs on the tailgate were echoed inside the Nomad with ribbing visible on the headliner.

(above) As Bunkie Knudsen said, you can sell an old man a young man's car, but not the other way around. The Bonneville exuded everything young, fresh, and powerful.

The huge bench seat offered nothing in the way of lateral support, but the 1957 Bonneville was a sedate handler, more suited for wafting down the Interstate.

1957 Pontiac Bonneville Specs
Wheelbase: 124 inches
Price: $5,782
Total built: 630 production, 3 prototypes
Available fuel injection: 315 horsepower

(above) With its massive chrome-plated front, the 1957 Bonneville was bold and unmistakably sporty. Fourteen-inch wheels gave the vehicle a lower look.

Looking like the business end of a missile, the Bonneville embraced the concept that if some chrome is good, lots of chrome is great.

Pontiac took a big step toward the low, wide, and long look with the 1957 Catalina. Overnight, *performance* and *Pontiac* belonged in the same sentence.

Chevrolet's engineers have always gotten credit for the ingenious stamped rocker arms that were inexpensive to manufacture and lightened the valve train, allowing for higher engine rpm. Actually, it was Pontiac's engine group that created the stamped rocker arm for its V-8 engine. Chevrolet's engineers were quick to see the benefits and added them to the V-8 they introduced in 1955.

With a big car comes a big engine compartment, and Pontiac used all that space to stuff in a beefy 347-cubic-inch V-8, including a NASCAR-certified "extra-horsepower" option.

As befitting an upscale division, Pontiac equipped the Catalina with plenty of flash and fun. There was no shortage of brightwork in the comfortable interior.

Looking like it was pulled from a rocket, the taillight assembly on the big Pontiac left people staring in its wake.

Looking like a concept car that escaped from GM's styling studio, this high-end Eldorado was rare (1,800 built) and expensive ($7,286).

General Motors debuted the Eldorado name, meaning "Golden One," in 1952 on a concept car celebrating the company's 50th anniversary. A fresh design in 1957 based on the Series 62, the sloping trunk is flanked by modest fins. Cadillac ads at the time noted that the 1957s were "brilliantly new in beauty, brilliantly new in performance!" *Photos by Mike Mueller*

In an era when too much was just enough, the Eldorado Biarritz showed considerable restraint. The interior was tastefully appointed in rich materials and high build quality.

All Eldorados were fitted with the beefy 365-cubic-inch V-8, rated at 325 horsepower, thanks to dual four-barrel carburetors.

(right) Low and wide was the clarion call for the 1958 Chevrolet. This body style was a one-year-only affair, unheard of today.

(below) In a trend that would last for the next fifteen years, Chevrolet boosted the power on its V-8 line, as bragging rights on a Saturday night became all important.

For 1958 Chevrolet created an X-frame design. This departure from the typical perimeter frame allowed for lower floors resulting in a lower profile overall for the vehicle. In 1965, Chevrolet abandoned this design and went back to the perimeter frame, which gave the cars greater rigidity and didn't require a two-piece driveshaft.

(above) Vestigial fins hinted at what was to come, while Chevrolet stylists tried to one-up Chrysler's designers for wild sheet metal.

'58 CHEVROLET

The 1958 Chevrolet Impala in Anniversary Gold, a new color created in commemoration of General Motors 50th Anniversary Year.

The biggest, boldest move any car ever made! *For more about it, turn the page...*

(Left) As the battle for over-the-top body design raged, the interiors of 1958 Detroit iron grew more vivid, including the 1958 Impala.

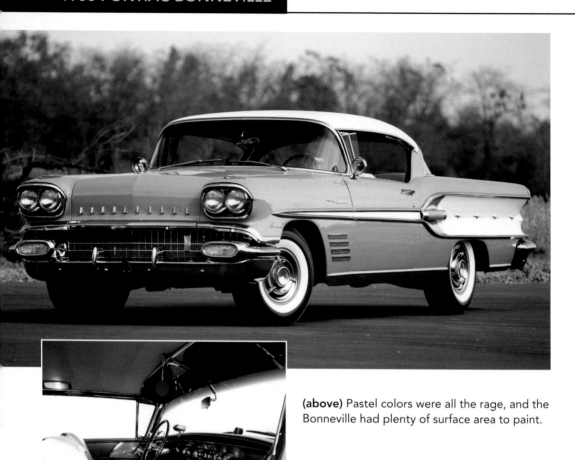

(above) Pastel colors were all the rage, and the Bonneville had plenty of surface area to paint.

With bucket seats, sparkle carpet, and door-to-door chrome, the interior would dazzle the most jaded motorist.

Pontiac had a 5.1 percent market share in 1958, with a model-year production of 217,303 units. A Tri-Power–equipped Bonneville paced the 1958 Indianapolis 500-Mile Race.

Quad headlights debuted in 1958 in an effort to modernize the Bonneville's appearance.

(above) Faux vents, "rocket" exhaust ports, chrome spears, and fender wings lent a Jet-Age air to the ground-bound Pontiac.

(above) As a subset of the Bel Air line, the big Chevrolet Bel Air Impala was a one-year-only design. Lower, wider, and heavier, it showed where Detroit was heading, in a hurry.

Four-bulb headlights debuted on the 1958 Chevrolet, giving the vehicle no small amount of "Cadillac" feel.

The Impala name made its debut in 1958 as an upscale trim level to the Bel Air line. It wouldn't be until 1961 that the Impala debuted as a separate line. New for 1958 was a 348-cubic-inch V-8, a big-block that could generate up to 315 horsepower. Starting cost for the Bel Air Impala convertible was $2,724.

(right) Multi-colored inserts were part of the Impala interior trim package. Per the styling trend of the time: When in doubt, add chrome!

(below) Giving the interior a sporting touch was the steering wheel, complete with "lightening" holes, as found on race cars. The full-width brightwork emphasized the 77.7-inch width.

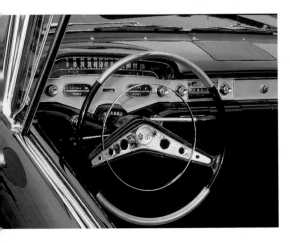

(above) Looking poised for take-off, the 1959 Chevrolet borrowed heavily from the aerospace industry for its winged, scooped, and thrust-line look.

In 1959, Chevrolet offered two different displacement V-8s in a wide range of horsepower ratings. This large selection of engines came about because cars were getting heavier, the interstate highway system was luring more drivers to the high-speed lanes, and buyers were finding they enjoyed the passing power of a few extra horsepower.

Four Tri-Power induction systems were available to the buyer in 1959. The biggest difference was how fast you wanted to get a ticket.

(above) Riding on a huge 119-inch wheelbase, the 1959 Chevrolet soaked up road imperfections with ease. However, spirited cornering was just a dream.

(left) Not for the shy, the interior of the 1959 Chevrolet was bold, bright, and big. Detroit was determined to supply the buying public with as much flash as they could swallow.

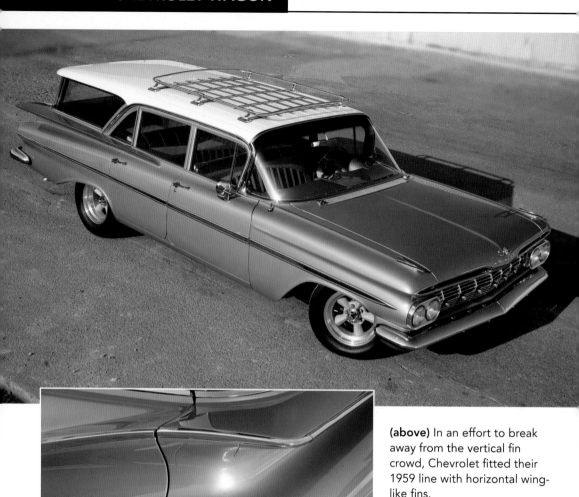

(above) In an effort to break away from the vertical fin crowd, Chevrolet fitted their 1959 line with horizontal wing-like fins.

Riding on a 119-inch wheelbase, the full-sized Chevrolets of 1959 wore a "Slimline Design" body, and 1959 saw the introduction of Magic Mirror acrylic lacquer.

Not an effectively aerodynamic design, the 1959 Chevrolet more than made up for it with stunning visuals.

(above) Load the back with vacation gear, toss the kids in the back seat, and point the long Chevrolet toward the beach. See the USA indeed!

The 348-cubic-inch V-8 offered four levels of performance with the impressive Tri-Power induction system.

(above) All new for 1959, the Catalina was the rolling embodiment of "lower, longer, wider."

Built on a long 122-inch wheelbase, the Catalina could fill the largest garage. Popular with customers, Pontiac built 231,561 in 1959. The motoring press thought highly of the car, as *Motor Trend* awarded Pontiac the famous Car of the Year trophy.

A big car demands a big engine, and the Catalina's 389-cubic-inch V-8 certainly qualified. Power ranged from 245 to 280 horsepower.

One of the benefits of a full-sized platform is having a full-sized interior. The Catalina could transport the entire clan in comfort.

Riding on a huge 130-inch wheelbase, the Eldorado measured 225 inches from end to end. New for 1959 was a jewel-patterned grille, a real pain to clean.

The long, low Eldorado tipped the scales at 5,060 pounds, yet the air suspension allowed it to swallow road imperfections with ease. Production was low, with 1,320 made, yet the vehicle's influence on the automotive scene was huge. To this day, it is regarded as one of the most desirable vehicles from the 1950s. *Photos by Mike Mueller*

Standard in the Eldorado engine compartment was a 390-cubic-inch V-8 rated at 325 horse-power with a single four-barrel carburetor.

One of the most iconic automotive styling cues, the huge tail fins on the 1959 Cadillac Eldorado marked the high-water mark for such extravagant design.

Ford, Mercury, Lincoln, and Edsel

Ford, Mercury, Lincoln, and Edsel

The Ford name and Ford cars are legendary in automotive history. Henry Ford perfected the assembly line for automobile production, developed the first practical V-8 engine, and recognized the benefit of making cars for the masses. In the years leading up to the 1950s, the Lincoln and Mercury division were added to provide luxury and mid-price cars to the company's lineup. Ford entered the 1950s with cars they had redesigned for the late 1940s. They were solidly built but not as stylish or powerful as any of the cars they would offer later in the decade. By the mid-1950s, Ford was producing a dynamic sports car and had another mid-size car on the drawing board. Unfortunately that car, the Edsel, became synonymous with failure.

Ford

The Ford name, along with its blue oval logo, had become one of the most trusted companies in American history. Since its first days in business, Ford delivered millions of cars to put America on wheels. The 1950s would be no different, as Ford continued to build on its legacy of producing excellent cars.

Previous spread: 1959 Ford Galaxie Skyliner

In 1949, Ford delivered a new car that eliminated all vestiges of running boards and 1930s designs. This new car was a gamble in that it was completely new and included such improvements as a fully independent front suspension and an open driveline. It rode 3 inches lower than the 1948 model, to which it bore no family resemblance. The 1949 Ford still used the trusty but dated flathead engine, but since every car in its price class was only running a six, it led the low-price field. Ford carried the basic 1949 body through 1951 with only minor changes, the biggest of which was a true hardtop for 1951.

For 1952, Ford's design team created an attractive car that bore little similarity to the 1951 model. Its contemporary design features included a one-piece windshield, attractive round taillights, and large false air scoops on each quarter panel. Ford would carry this attractive body style through the end of the 1954 model year. In 1954, they officially retired the flathead V-8 and replaced it with a new overhead design that displaced 239 cubic inches. Before the end of the decade, the engine would be displacing 272 and then 312 cubic inches. In 1954, Ford introduced the Skyliner hardtop that included a Plexiglas insert over the front seats.

In 1955, Ford again completely redesigned its car lines. The new Ford featured sleek contemporary lines with attractive side chrome moldings that worked well to divide the body for the popular two-tone paint schemes. Ford also introduced the Thunderbird in 1955 that, by design, had a strong family resemblance to its full-size Fairlane brother. Ford introduced a new model for 1955, the Crown Victoria, which featured an attractive stainless band wrapped over the roof between angled B-pillars. The Crown Vic was also on the option list for face-lifted 1956 Ford models.

Competition from Chevrolet in 1955 and 1956 had been brutal. To counter for 1957, Ford's designers pulled out all the stops to create an exceptionally attractive car. It featured a full-width grille and slender tail fins. Ford also released the Skyliner, with its first retractable hardtop. It gave the customer both the comfort of a hardtop and the fun of a convertible. Ford outsold Chevrolet in 1957, something it hadn't done in many years.

Like all automakers, Ford suffered during the 1958 economic recession. Sales dropped from 1.7 million in 1957 to just under 1 million in 1958. Ford introduced the four-seat Thunderbird that became an instant hit. Ford also continued to make the retractable hardtop Skyliner, but in fewer numbers than in 1957. They also introduced two new "FE" series engines, one that displaced 332 cubic inches and another that displaced 352 cubic inches.

For 1959, Ford re-skinned its full-size car line. Mid-year, it introduced the Galaxie series of hardtops and sedans. Ford could also boast about its smooth-shifting three-speed Cruise-O-Matic automatic transmission.

Ford did well in the 1950s. The management team created attractive cars and kept pace with innovations in technology. They introduced the Thunderbird and—against all odds—cut short the two-seat version to produce a four-seat model, thus creating the first personal luxury car. Ford developed several new V-8 engines in the 1950s and a retractable hardtop. Ford even outsold Chevrolet for one year in 1957.

Lincoln

In 1922, Henry Ford bought the Lincoln Motorcar Company. Throughout the 1930s, Henry's son, Edsel, nurtured the Lincoln model into an honored luxury brand. Following World War II, the Lincoln's well-rounded design looked like a larger Mercury. This design would be carried through 1951.

For 1952, Ford's design team reshaped the Lincoln into a sleek, sophisticated car. It carried enough of the Mercury's styling cues to keep the family heritage intact. In addition to the stylish new body, Ford's engineers added the powerful new 317-cubic-inch V-8 (the first of the V-block series) and a ball-joint front suspension. The new Lincolns also offered a long list of luxury options, including power seats and air conditioning. The new 1952 Lincoln fit well into the selection of upscale cars offered that year.

The term "hot rod Lincoln" must have been coined in 1952 when Lincolns made an impressive showing at the Carrera Panamericana, a road race across Mexico. Ford engineers added special components to make the Lincolns faster and more durable. Between 1952 and 1954, the Lincoln models entered were the class of the field.

Ford redesigned the Lincoln for 1955, and the first glimpses of tail fins were seen. They also increased the V-8's displacement to 341 cubic inches to help tote around the extra weight. As good as the new Lincoln was, it sold poorly in an otherwise hot car market. The lightly redesigned 1956 models sold well, but sales of the Lincoln were still far behind those of Cadillac, the luxury car benchmark of the 1950s.

Four-door hardtops were among the hot body styles in 1957, and Lincoln's completely redesigned models featured one. The redesign also included large tail fins, something every 1957 model seemed to have. Lincoln's designers also added vertically stacked quad headlights, a design feature that would be widely seen in 1958 but was considered cutting edge in 1957. As good as the 1957 looked, it could not crack the code of Cadillac and big car buyers. For 1958, Ford invested millions on an all-new Lincoln in an attempt to capture that elusive market.

When Ford created the 1958 Lincoln, engineers designed and built a car that was bigger than anything on the road. This unitized chassis behemoth rode on a 131-inch wheelbase and was fitted with the largest-displacement engine of the era—430 cubic inches that developed 375 horsepower. The styling featured heavily sculpted sides, slanted quad headlights, and huge bumpers. But sales of the 1958 Lincolns and the equally big 1959 models were poor. Lincoln would rebound in the 1960s with a series of more appropriately designed cars.

The elegant 1956 and 1957 Mark II is a glamorous footnote to the Lincolns of the 1950s. Ford designed it to represent the elegance of the cars from the '20s and '30s, when movie stars drove Duesenbergs or Pierce Arrows. The Lincoln Mark II featured hand-built craftsmanship with a price to match ($10,000). After producing only 3,012 units over a two-year period, Ford decided that the Lincoln Mark II was not cost effective, so it was canceled.

Mercury

Mercury also benefited from Ford's total redesign of its model line for 1949. The Mercury resembled the 1949 Lincoln with its inverted bathtub look and smooth lines. Engineers carried this basic design through 1951. When Ford redesigned its entire line again in 1952, the Mercury once again benefited from its resemblance to the Lincoln. Mercury was also helped by the addition of the pillar-less hardtop design that Ford added to all of its cars for 1952. While not revolutionary, it turned what would have been a mundane two-door sedan into a sportier-looking car.

In 1954, Mercury dropped the ancient flathead for its version of the new Y-block V-8. Mercury's chassis engineers added a ball-joint front suspension to the 1954 models. The Sun Valley hardtop, with its Plexiglas roof panel, gave dealers an attractive feature to show potential customers. The Sun Valley's tinted panel covered the front half of the roof, giving the driver a protected and unobstructed view of the sky. Mercury included a snap-in shade to keep the interior cooler on exceptionally sunny days. Although this was an interesting option, the public bought only 9,761 of them. Mercury offered the Sun Valley option again in 1955 with its restyled product line, but with even fewer sales than in 1954, the model was discontinued.

In 1956, Mercury added a four-door hardtop, a body style that consumers were anxious to see. Mercury designers added an attractive "Z" molding to the side of the 1956 models that gave them the freedom to explore new and inventive options for two-tone paint schemes. The engine group added to the Mercury performance ledger by increasing the Y-block displacement to 312 cubic inches.

Mercury pulled out all the stops for 1957. The Mercury cars now rode on a unique 122-inch wheelbase chassis and featured a new sculpted body with massive bumpers. The Turnpike Cruiser was an added model that featured plenty of gimmicks, including horizontally mounted antennas above the A-pillar and a rearward-slanting rear window that could be rolled down. Designers also featured the use of gold anodized side trim, another material that was becoming fashionable for cars in the late 1950s. But the new design did nothing to help sales, as Mercury fell from seventh to eighth place. The 1958 recession hurt sales even more on the revamped Mercury, during a time when all mid-range cars experienced poor sales.

For 1959, Mercury designers rolled out a much bigger car that now rode on a 126-inch wheelbase. The Turnpike Cruiser was no longer part of the simplified model lineup. They also dropped the higher-horsepower engines that had been a hallmark of Mercury cars in the previous years. Sales again flagged, with Mercury only delivering 150,000 cars in 1959. But with muscle cars taking center stage in the 1960s, Mercury would make a strong comeback.

Edsel

Ford Motor Company released the new Edsel, named in honor of company founder Henry Ford's son, to great fanfare in 1958. It was also in the heart of the first major economic recession since World War II. It was simply the wrong car at the wrong time.

Ford's strong recovery in the early 1950s allowed the manufacturer to experiment with new designs. This led to the Thunderbird and the search for another mid-priced car to compliment its lineup. General Motors had Buick, Pontiac, and Oldsmobile in between Chevrolet and Cadillac, but Ford offered only the Mercury. Another mid-size model at a time when the sales of mid-size cars were booming seemed like the right thing to do.

Ford engineers borrowed heavily from the Mercury to create the Edsel. The design staff added some unique touches that would make it stand out, including gull-wing taillights and the now-infamous horse-collar grille. The Ford family was against using Edsel's name on the car, but relented. Ford's original concept was a car between a Mercury and Lincoln, but the Edsel ended up being just a step above a Ford.

The 1958 Edsel could be bought in four models on two different chassis. The Ranger and Pacer rode on a 118-inch wheelbase chassis and the upscale Corsair and Citation used Mercury's 124-inch wheelbase chassis. The Ranger and Pacer were fitted with a 361-cubic-inch, 303-horsepower engine and the Corsair and Citation owners were treated to a standard 410-cubic-inch, 345-horsepower engine. The new Edsel was also fitted with a host of gadgets, including a pushbutton transmission selector mounted in the center of the steering wheel and a kitschy drum-type speedometer. The new 1958 Edsel ranged in price from $2,500 to $3,800—about $500 below a comparably equipped Mercury.

Even though outrageous styling was the norm in 1958, the Edsel never won the hearts of America's car buyers. It also had its share of mechanical problems and was soon taking pot shots from every automotive journalist. Ford's new Edsel Division had projected sales of 100,000 for its '58 model but missed that mark by 40,000. Edsel's executives were smart enough to cut the 1959 model offerings to two: Ranger and Corsair, which were simply re-skinned Fords. Edsel's designers toned down the excesses of 1958, but it was still tough for the public to get past that grille. The short-lived 1960s models were obviously re-badged Fords. Before the end of 1959, Ford Motor Company pulled the plug on the 1960s Edsel.

Had Ford introduced the Edsel a few years earlier or later it may have been a success. Unfortunately, today the name of Henry Ford's only son is forever attached to a car that failed critically and financially. The Edsel became the poster child for the ailing auto industry and the butt of jokes for years to come. For the next couple of decades, it also made Ford think twice about taking a chance on anything new and different.

With the exception of the Edsel, Ford did exceptionally well in the 1950s. Sales of its car lines did well, as they introduced new engines and lots of gadgetry to keep the buyers' attention. The highpoint had to have been the introduction of the Thunderbird (see Chapter 4) and its subsequent metamorphosis into a four-passenger luxury car.

Looking ready to take a scientist to safety from a mutant ant or spider or scorpion, the 1954 Ford had inoffensive styling and solid engineering.

Ford first offered a low-cost V-8 in its 1932 Ford passenger car. This flathead design served them well through the 1953 model year. In 1954, Ford introduced its first overhead-valve engine affectionately called the "Y" block. The deep-skirted design of this block provided exceptional support to the crankshaft.

From its oil-bath air filter to the bottom of the oil pan, the 1954 Ford used an all-new V-8, displacing 239 cubic inches.

The clean design seen on the 1954 Ford was soon to give way to increasingly outrageous styling. This mid-'50s Ford quietly shouted stability and good taste.

Nothing fancy, but it got the job done. However, it wouldn't be long before customers demanded to be wowed by the interior.

With two doors and seating for six, the Ranch Wagon was beach ready. The Ranch Wagon was part of the Mainline family of vehicles.

Ford installed a 223-cubic-inch, 115-horsepower, straight six-cylinder engine as standard. But the optional 239-cubic-inch, 130-horsepower V-8 offered a quicker drive.

Chevrolet was not the only manufacturer to offer a two-door wagon in the 1950s. In fact, the Ford Ranch Wagon was first released in 1952. The 3,338-pound vehicle sold in respectable numbers in 1954, to the tune of 44,315 units. That figure takes into account both six- and eight-cylinder engines. *Photos by Mike Mueller*

Restrained styling was the norm in the entire 1954 Ford lineup, including the Ranch Wagon.

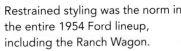

Beneath the oil-bath air cleaner lived a two-barrel Holley carburetor.

Ford "borrowed" the swooping side spear from the 1955 Thunderbird concept car and grafted it onto the side of the new 1955 Crown Victoria.

Circular taillights and small fins made the rear of the 1955 Crown Victoria look like a large Thunderbird, maintaining a familial presence.

Starting in 1955, Ford and Chevrolet increased their intense competition for the low end of the market by providing new models and cars with upgraded content. Both companies offered sports cars, a V-8 engine, and a wide range of beautiful passenger cars. Topping the list of cars were Chevrolet's high-end Nomad wagon and Ford's attractive Crown Victoria.

Ford slipped a 115.5-inch wheelbase beneath the 1955 Crown Victoria, giving it good cruising characteristics while maintaining good handling.

Ford laid the instrument panel out in a no-nonsense fashion in the 1955 Crown Victoria. It wouldn't be long before simplicity would go out the window.

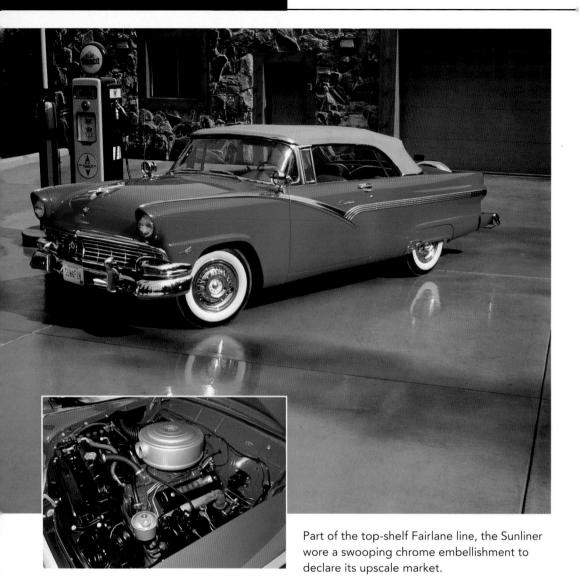

Part of the top-shelf Fairlane line, the Sunliner wore a swooping chrome embellishment to declare its upscale market.

Ford depended on the 312-cubic-inch V-8's 215 horsepower to get this Sunliner down the road.

The 1956 Ford lineup was essentially carried over from 1955. The Sunliner was a popular model, with 58,147 units sold. The fair-weather ride weighed in at 3,455 pounds.

Photos by Mike Mueller

Wire wheel covers set off the liberal use of chrome throughout the car and lent a sporty touch.

As the Sunliner was slotted in at the top of the Ford lineup, the interior enjoyed a rich mixture of materials and eye-pleasing brightwork.

The 1957 Turnpike Cruiser was powered by a 290-horsepower, 368-cubic-inch V-8. It topped out at 120 miles per hour and tipped the scales at 4,100 pounds

At the 1956 auto shows, the public saw the XM Turnpike Cruiser, the precursor to the production car in 1957. Equipped with dual skylights, a pushbutton Merc-O-Matic transmission, and a memory seat with 49 positions, Mercury whet the public's appetite for conspicuous consumption.

Beauty shared by no other car—biggest size and value increase in the industry

FAMILY-CAR SIZE
There's stretch-out comfort for six. This year's Mercury is bigger in 8 vital dimensions inside, 4 outside. There are inches of spare headroom, hip room, shoulder room, and leg room.

PRICED FOR EASY BUYING
Never before has so much bigness and luxury cost so little. See for yourself. Ask your nearby dealer for the fun-to-read figures, today.

ONLY MERCURY OFFERS YOU THESE 6 DREAM-CAR FEATURES
• Exclusive Dream-Car Design
• Exclusive Floating Ride, with 4 new bump-smothering features
• Exclusive Power-Booster Fan in Montclair Series
• New Merc-O-Matic Keyboard Control
• Power seat that "remembers"
• New Thermo-Matic Carburetor

EXCLUSIVE DREAM-CAR DESIGN. Here is sleek-lined beauty, a massive grace, that is Mercury's alone. Notice the distinctive Jet-Flo bumpers, V-angle tail-lights.

THE BIG MERCURY for '57 *with DREAM-CAR DESIGN*

MERCURY DIVISION • FORD MOTOR COMPANY

Measuring 211.1 inches long and loaded with an abundance of gadgets and distinct 1950s styling, it was ready to tackle the growing Interstate Highway system. Note the optional "Dream-Car Spare Tire Carrier," a.k.a., a continental tire kit.

Mercury fitted the strong 368-cubic-inch V-8 into the Turnpike Cruiser, rated at 290 horsepower at 4,600 rpm and 405 lb-ft of torque at 2,800 revs.

Pure Jet Age, the aerials jutting forward at the top of the windshield were for show only, but what a rolling feast for the eyes.

With its "horse-collar" grille, the Edsel looked like no other vehicle in its debut year. It was meant to fit in between the Mercury and Lincoln lines.

With 345 horsepower surging from the 410-cubic-inch V-8, getting the power to the ground through the narrow tires was a challenge.

The public panned the Edsel in the showroom, to the tune of only 63,110 built in the model year. The Edsel would only last three years before Ford halted production and swept it from sight.

The taillights had a "squinting" appearance on the trailing edge of the tail fins. Like most automobiles in the 1950s, the trunk was very generous, able to swallow an entire family's vacation luggage.

The Edsel enjoyed high-grade interior materials in an effort to position the vehicle in an up-market spot.

Period advertisements noted that, "The man who owns a Lincoln drives a car of classic beauty." In the fine print it was noted that "Mark III prices are just slightly above the fine car field."

Looking like it rolled out of a scene in *North by Northwest*, the Mk III was a headturner. While some scorned the headlight treatment, there was no denying that the big Lincoln was unmistakable. Lincoln built 3,048 convertibles. Unfortunately, a recession cost Lincoln sales. The wheelbase measured 131 inches, while the overall length was a garage-filling 229 inches. That's 19 feet! *Photos by Mike Mueller*

Motivating the Continental Mk III was a huge 430-cubic-inch V-8, rated at 375 horsepower. With its 10.5:1 compression, premium fuel (and lots of it) was a must.

Plush, roomy, and stylish, the Continental's interior spoke of money well spent, to the tune of $6,223.

Canted headlights debuted on the 1958 Mk III and were meant to differentiate it from its Cadillac competition.

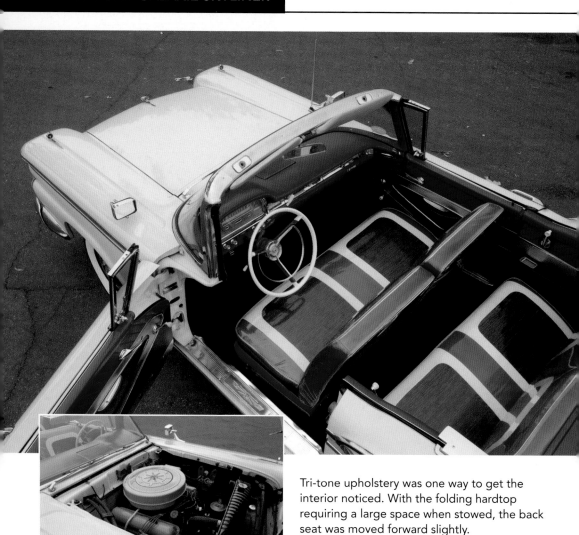

Tri-tone upholstery was one way to get the interior noticed. With the folding hardtop requiring a large space when stowed, the back seat was moved forward slightly.

With 3,527 pounds on the tires, it was necessary to have a V-8 beneath the hood.

Ford's lineup won a Gold Medal for Exceptional Styling at the 1959 Brussels World Fair. While its Detroit competitors were fitting their vehicles with ever larger fins and more chrome, Ford took a restrained approach to its designs, with beautiful results.

The folding hardtop left little room in the trunk when stowed, but it was decades ahead of its time. Today, a folding hardtop is considered the latest innovation.

The back-up lamps in the tips of the fins only came on when the headlights were in operation. Huge taillights resemble jet afterburners—no doubt, just a coincidence.

Chrysler

Chrysler

I n 1949, Chrysler President Tex Colbert brought crack designer Virgil Exner in to head the company's Advanced Studio. Exner wrestled the development of new car styling away from the engineers and placed it in the hands of designers. Soon after, the auto shows featured Chrysler "Idea Cars," exotic machines like the Chrysler d'Elegance, the DeSoto Adventurer, and the Dodge Firearrow. Designed in Detroit, these cars of the future were built by Italian coachbuilder Ghia. Exner favored the beauty of European designs, which he felt had evolved from elegant coaches used by European royalty. All of Chrysler's products in the 1950s benefited from Exner's sophisticated design touch.

Chrysler

Chrysler introduced its first V-8 engine in 1951. Chrysler's new Hemi Firepower V-8 developed 180 horsepower and was only available in New Yorker, Imperial, and Saratoga models. Chrysler's Hemi engine was so named because of its hemispherical combustion chamber. This combustion chamber design is exceptionally efficient because of its minimal surface area and valve placement.

Exner's partiality to the clean European lines led to a minimal amount of chrome. This was contrary to the mid-1950s trend toward extra chrome. Exner determined that the new C-300, so named for the 300-horsepower Hemi engine under the hood, would be produced in only three basic colors: Black, Platinum White, and Tango Red.

While Chrysler's engineers worked under the hood, its excellent team of designers (led by Virgil Exner) were creating some of the most dynamic designs of the era. The 1955 Chrysler C-300 created a reversal of trends by eliminating the abundance of chrome being applied to the exterior. This ground-breaking car also featured a special heavy-duty suspension that lowered the car by 1 inch and included optional chrome wire wheels.

In 1956, America's most powerful car got even more powerful and was now designated the 300B. Chrysler's designers added new quarter panels featuring sleek fins to satisfy the public's desires. The 1956 300B retained the same minimalist approach to exterior ornamentation while providing maximum performance. The front of the 1956 300B changed very little from the 1955 C-300.

Previous spread: 1957 Chrysler 300C

The culmination of Chrysler's 1950s design excellence had to be the 1957 Chrysler 300C, which led the parade of stunning vehicles. Chrysler gambled that the buying public would welcome the dramatic changes to its product line.

Once again the Chrysler 300C had the distinction of being the most powerful car on the road, as well as one of the most beautiful. Available as either a convertible or a hardtop, the 1957 300C strutted its clean lines, which ran from its crisp quad headlights to a pair of lofty tail fins. While designers added more chrome to other Chrysler models, they restricted the use of chrome on the 300C to a thin quarter-panel molding that ended in a round, tri-color 300C emblem.

Chrysler's designers gave the 1959 300E a face-lift, but they failed to preserve the sleek lines of the earlier versions. They replaced the egg-crate grille insert with one featuring four slender horizontal bars. They added a massive rear bumper and simply changed the taillights. In an effort to give the car a new look, designers added chrome molding to the rocker panel and the rear wheel lip. These modifications had little merit in terms of styling or practicality and did nothing to advance the clean lines of the earlier C and D models.

Engineers worked under the hood to make big changes in the 1959 300E. They introduced a new generation of wedge engine, thereby ending the Hemi's muscular reign. But Chrysler didn't emasculate the car completely. The less-expensive wedge engine still offered 380 horsepower—the level of performance expected by a 300 letter-series owner.

Through the 1950s, Chrysler created a legend with its 300-series cars. They were superbly designed and offered some of the most powerful engines of the decade. They set the trend with attractive fins while bucking the trend of excessive chrome and two-tone paint schemes.

Imperial

In 1955, Chrysler Corporation decided that the Imperial should no longer just be a model of Chrysler but a separate and distinct make. It would be obvious to the car buyer that there was still a family resemblance between Chrysler and Imperial, but the separation allowed Imperial to create its own identity and add more content to its cars.

The 1955 and 1956 Imperials were elegant cars. They were based on Exner's earlier show cars and featured a unique gun-sight taillight that sat on top of the quarter panel. Under the hood was a Chrysler Hemi engine backed by a standard automatic transmission.

In 1957, Imperial's designers followed through with the second generation of Forward Look designs. The gun-sight taillights remained, but they were now nestled into large fins. On the technical side, the 1957 Imperial improved measurably with the addition of the TorqueFlite transmission and torsion bar front suspension. Chrysler would improve the 1957 model for 1958 and again for 1959. Though the changes were minor in terms of content, they were much touted by Chrysler.

DeSoto

In 1928, when Chrysler announced its plans to build a new model called the DeSoto, more than 500 dealers immediately signed up. By the end of 1929, there were 1,500 DeSoto dealers, and sales were at record levels. Chrysler positioned the DeSoto between the high-end Chrysler and the low-end Plymouth. The postwar DeSoto's boxy styling remained until 1955, when DeSoto was swept up in the tsunami of Chrysler's Forward Look redesign movement. Sales jumped 85 percent.

DeSoto introduced its first Firedome Hemi engine in 1952, producing 160 horsepower. By 1955, when the Forward Look DeSotos hit the streets, customers had two 291-cubic-inch Hemi engines from which to choose: one rated at 185 horsepower and the other rated at 200 horsepower. DeSoto officially jumped on Chrysler's performance bandwagon with the February 18, 1956, introduction of the Adventurer, a two-door hardtop with a high-performance engine and special trim. Its 341-cubic-inch Hemi featured dual quads, a high-performance camshaft, and dual exhaust. A special "Pacesetter" convertible version paced the 1956 Indianapolis 500.

DeSoto's 1956 testing of the performance waters paid off with a much more refined Adventurer model for 1957. The new DeSoto also benefited from Chrysler's complete "Flight Sweep" redesign of the series. It was lower and longer with graceful tail fins. The Adventurer was conspicuously absent during the initial introduction of the new 1957 DeSoto lineup on October 30, 1956. When it made its appearance two months later, the new Adventurer was an instant hit. The gold-colored accents returned, along with a host of standard features, including power brakes, TorqueFlite transmission, dual exhausts, and white sidewall tires. With 345 horsepower from 345 cubic inches, the Adventurer's powerful engine matched its dynamic styling.

Dodge

The Dodge division had been a part of Chrysler since 1928. People had come to know and trust the brand as providing good cars that were a step above Plymouth in size, styling, and amenities. The cars Dodge marketed between 1950 and 1952 were for the most part carried over from the 1948 redesigns. Dodge executives were keenly tuned into the fact that they needed a V-8 to continue to compete in the market.

Based on the Chrysler Hemi V-8, Dodge named its new engine the Red Ram. In 1953, this 241-cubic-inch engine developed 140 horsepower. The upside to the Hemi engine is its ability to easily develop lots of horsepower; the downsides are the cost of manufacturing and the weight of the engine.

In 1954, Dodge made its new V-8 available in all of its models. Dodge saw an opportunity to break out of its stodgy mold with the new 150-horsepower Hemi V-8 fitted into its new sporty Royal line. Pacing the Indy 500 in 1954 was a yellow Royal 500 convertible. Dodge quickly created 701 pace car replicas to promote its new performance image.

The success of the 1955 Chrysler C-300 provided a new business model for Dodge in 1956. Dodge jumped into the performance sedan arena with its D-500, a complete engine-chassis package. This option was available for any of the new 1956 Dodge body styles but was best suited to the sleek hardtops and convertibles. Included with the D-500 option was the powerful 315-cubic-inch Red Ram Hemi engine, rated at 260 horsepower.

The 1957 Dodge benefited from Virgil Exner's keen eye and artistic hand. The Dodge made a quantum leap in styling with extraordinary rear fins positioned on a lower, sleeker body. In 1957, the D-500 option included a 325-cubic-inch Red Ram Hemi engine that produced 285 horsepower. Dodge offered a three-speed manual transmission as standard equipment, with the TorqueFlite automatic as a $220 option.

Engines were the biggest news for Dodge in 1958. Three V-8s were on the option list and only the 325-cubic-inch engine was a carryover. Like Plymouth, Dodge saw the extended virtue of the soon-to-be corporate "B" block and used two versions—one displacing 350 cubic inches and the other 361 cubic inches. The selection of the D-500 option in 1958 added one of the following 361-cubic-inch engines: a 305-horsepower model equipped with a single four-barrel carburetor or a 320-horsepower model equipped with dual quads.

For 1959, Dodge retained and improved the D-500 option. The base D-500 engine was equipped with a single four-barrel carburetor and produced 320 horsepower. The Super D-500 raised the horsepower bar to 345 with the help of twin Carter AFB carburetors. Other than the small "500" emblem on the side of the fins, the only indications that a 1959 Dodge was equipped with the D-500 option were the roar from the dual chrome exhaust tips under the rear bumper and the cloud of dust left hanging in the air as the sleek Dodge sped past.

Dodge developed a distinct personality in the 1950s. It grew from the performance image of the new Hemi engine and excellent styling. Dodge carried this success well into the 1960s.

Plymouth

Plymouth began the decade of the 1950s with warmed-over 1949 models, but things changed in 1955 when Plymouth broke out of its stodgy mold and started to produce exciting cars. The genesis of this change took place on the tip of designer Virgil Exner's pencil, where stylish sweeping lines replaced square-edged ones. Chrysler's "Forward Look" campaign filtered down to its lowest-priced sedan. This move was the kiss that turned the frog into a prince.

Fins came to America with a flourish in 1956 with the new Plymouth. With a forward-leaning nose and tall tail fins, the car looked like a U.S. Air Force F-86 Saber jet on wheels. On January 7, 1956, Plymouth spiced up the recipe by introducing a new top-of-the-line model, known as the Fury—a special high-performance coupe based on the Belvedere, which was Plymouth's 1956 model carrying its highest level of trim. All 1956 Plymouth Fury models were two-door hardtops and were painted a solid Egg Shell White. The Fury's bold side trim highlighted the car's dramatic profile. Plymouth added a large tapered gold anodized panel on each side, surrounded by thin, chromed strips. This insert panel ran from the front fender to the rear of the car, with an abrupt step up at the rear that accentuated the bold tail fins. This extensive use of gold anodized trim was a first for the industry.

The new 1957 Plymouth was lower, wider, and looked longer than the 1956 model. It also sprouted the highest tail fins of any production car to date. The *e*volution of the 1957 Plymouth had become a *re*volution, and the results were outstanding. Plymouth engineers designed a new frame for the 1957 model. They lengthened the wheelbase by 3 inches and added torsion bar suspension to the front. This design, in combination with the addition of 14-inch wheels, resulted in a car that was slightly more than 2 inches lower than the 1956 model. The new Plymouth was almost 4 inches wider. The dynamic Fury returned in 1957 at the top of Plymouth's stylish lineup.

Subtle changes to the exterior of the 1958 Plymouth revealed little of what was going on under the hood. The Fury still held sway with the most powerful standard engine of any car in 1958—the dual-quad 318-cubic-inch engine rated at 290 horsepower. But there was also a completely new optional engine with even more power—the 350-cubic-inch "B" engine. Chrysler's B engine is distinguished by its deep skirt block design and front-mounted distributor. This new B engine, aptly named the "Golden Commando," with its dual four-barrel carburetors, developed 305 horsepower.

The 1958 Plymouth received a mild face-lift consisting of quad headlights, a new lower front valence panel, revised side trim, and new taillights. The Fury returned as a special Belvedere model, available only as a two-door hardtop. Designers retained the Fury's now signature hockey stick–shaped gold side trim, gold grille, and gold wheel covers.

In 1959, Plymouth's designers took the clean, classic lines of the 1957 and 1958 models and "busied" them up. In the front, designers gave the eyebrow over the headlights a depression between the lights and enlarged the grid of the anodized grille. They increased the flair of the tail fins and the neatly integrated taillight of the 1957, and 1958 Plymouths gave way to what looked like the result of aftermarket add-ons.

Many of the features on the 1959 Plymouth could be defined as novelty items. When gimmicks define a car, instead of solid styling and expert engineering, it is a clear sign of trouble. This fact was proven at the end of 1959 when Plymouth's market share dropped by 13 percent.

(above) Riding on a 131.5-inch wheelbase, the New Yorker convertible was a lot of car for a lot of money—in this case $3,238.

This was the last year for the venerable L-head straight-eight engine that burst onto the scene in 1930. Displacing 323.5 cubic inches, it generated 135 horsepower at a lazy 3,200 rpm.

Only 899 convertibles in the New Yorker/Windsor line were built in 1950, yet Chrysler had their best year ever up to that date, with 176,000 units sold in the model year, despite a three-month-long labor strike. Period advertisements touted the New Yorker as "Daringly re-styled to be the finest in the fine car field." This was the first year that electric window lifts were offered.

(above) Chrysler started the 1950s with a conservative approach to styling, as the New Yorker wore gently rounded contours and tasteful brightwork.

Art deco design was evident in the interior of the 1950 Chrysler New Yorker. With World War II just a handful of years in the past, designers tended to carry on with prewar styling motifs.

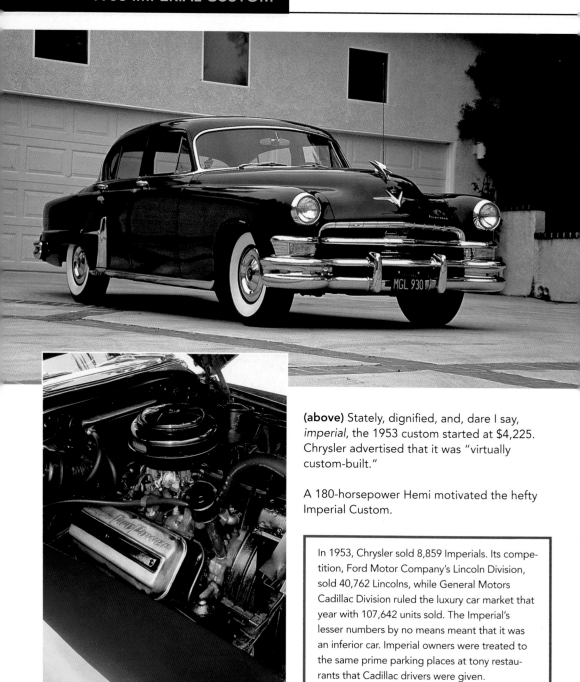

(above) Stately, dignified, and, dare I say, *imperial*, the 1953 custom started at $4,225. Chrysler advertised that it was "virtually custom-built."

A 180-horsepower Hemi motivated the hefty Imperial Custom.

In 1953, Chrysler sold 8,859 Imperials. Its competition, Ford Motor Company's Lincoln Division, sold 40,762 Lincolns, while General Motors Cadillac Division ruled the luxury car market that year with 107,642 units sold. The Imperial's lesser numbers by no means meant that it was an inferior car. Imperial owners were treated to the same prime parking places at tony restaurants that Cadillac drivers were given.

(above) Minimal flash and glitz were evident in the 1953 Imperial Custom, an upscale offering from Chrysler.

Restrained good taste was a hallmark of Imperial design in the first half of the 1950s.

The C-300 sat 1 inch lower than the other 1955 Chryslers due to its heavy-duty suspension.

The C-300 blended staggering power with unrivaled luxury, creating a true gentleman's express. Though it weighed 2 tons, its heavily modified Hemi churned out an honest 300 horsepower, enough to propel the vehicle at sustained triple-digit speeds. The heavy-duty suspension allowed the power to get to the ground in a controlled fashion.

The C-300 proved that an elegant and understated design could succeed in an era of flamboyant cars and color schemes. Good design never goes out of style.

(above) Very pricey at $4,665, the Imperial rode on a 130-inch wheelbase and was powered by the 331-Hemi Firepower V-8, rated at 250 horsepower.

Formal styling set the Imperial apart from virtually every other car on the road. The taillight treatment was pulled from the 1951 Chrysler K-310 concept car.

Chrysler touted the Imperial as "The Flagship of the FORWARD LOOK." Virgil Exner was a gifted designer, and Chrysler benefited from his talent. Like other expensive, high-end vehicles, production was low, only 3,418 Imperials being built. The body design was all-new for 1955.

Befitting its status as a top-shelf automobile, the Imperial carried a full slate of instrumentation. Power steering made maneuvering the huge car a snap.

Brightwork was heavily used, but with good taste. The name Chrysler did not appear on the vehicle; it was an Imperial by Chrysler.

From it split grille to its fin-like taillights, the station wagon never looked so good. As a Chrysler, it boasted quality materials; and as a wagon, it was rare, with only 1,036 built.

The New Yorker line was the best offered from Chrysler in 1955, and that mix of quality and station wagon functionality should have found more buyers. However, the typical New Yorker buyer was not the sort to toss a bale of hay into the back. These beautiful cars were intended for gracious horse farms and yacht clubs, where only the finest leather saddles and boating gear would sully the back.

118

Load up the kids and the dog, it's vacation time! Tipping the scales at 4,430 lbs, the big wagon delivered a smooth ride.

(left) Even though the Town & Country was a station wagon, it never forgot that it was also a Chrysler New Yorker. Plenty of chrome and brightwork teased the eye, while the rock-solid construction meant years of service.

(below) With its split, folding second-row seats, virtually any shape cargo would slide into the voluminous cabin.

(above) The 300B used its minimalist approach to exterior ornamentation to lull the unsuspecting, while delivering maximum performance.

It's hard to believe, but the full-sized 300B was the most powerful automobile for sale in 1956. It continued a tradition of roomy, comfortable, fast transportation, all the while wearing classy sheet metal.

While the 300B was essentially a carryover from 1955, a 340-horsepower Hemi is not a bad thing to carry over.

(above) Acres of leather beckoned passengers into the spacious interior of the 300B. What a great way to cross the country!

The front of the 1956 Chrysler 300B featured the same bold grille as the 1955 model, except for the addition of the letter "B" to the front emblem.

(above) Graceful, in an ocean-liner sort of way, the DeSoto used a staggering amount of chrome and brightwork to make a strong visual statement.

Few automakers held a candle to the 1957 DeSoto for sheer stylistic impact. Ford and GM would play catch-up in the ensuing years.

1956 DeSoto Prices:
Adventurer two-door hardtop: $3,678
Fireflite four-door hardtop: $3,341
Power steering: $97
Power brakes: $40
Power front seat: $70

(above) In the age when the engine was actually visible, it was all business under the hood.

A mixture of leather and brocade cloth gave the 1957 DeSoto an upscale look and feel.

(above) In 1956, DeSoto Fireflight prices started at $3,074, a substantial sum for the era.

In the 1950s even a large engine left plenty of room to work. Notice that the actual ground is visible, not an option with contemporary vehicles.

In addition to the special Pacesetter convertible, DeSoto also released the limited-edition Adventurer two-door hardtop. This car was often called the "Golden Adventurer" because of its gold-colored trim. DeSoto installed a dual-quad, 341-cubic-inch Hemi rated at 320 horsepower. One Adventurer paced the 1956 Pikes Peak Hill Climb, and another competed in the Daytona Speedweeks competition.

With a hemispherical combustion chamber, the 1956 DeSoto revved higher than other V-8 engines of its era.

Stylish comfort awaited the driver and passengers. Only a few hundred Indianapolis 500-Mile Race pace car replicas were built

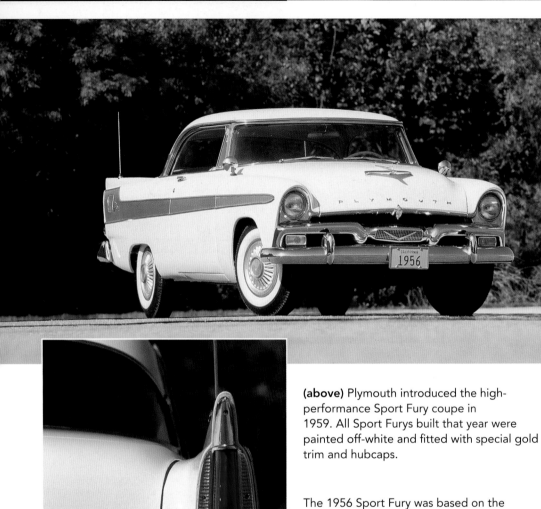

(above) Plymouth introduced the high-performance Sport Fury coupe in 1959. All Sport Furys built that year were painted off-white and fitted with special gold trim and hubcaps.

The 1956 Sport Fury was based on the Belvedere. Plymouth used gold anodized aluminum for the Fury's side molding.

By driving it like you stole it, the Fury would sprint to 60 miles per hour in 9.7 seconds and could cover the quarter-mile in 17 seconds—impressive numbers for the era. In period advertisements, the push was on the "Swept Wing 58 by Dodge."

The Fury Sport Coupe debuted in dealer showrooms on January 7, 1956. With a top speed of 124 miles per hour, quite a few motorists got this view of the swift Plymouth.

With a beefy 303-cubic-inch V-8 using 9.25:1 compression topped with two Carter four-barrel carburetors, the Sport Fury generated a stout 240 horsepower.

(above) Virgil Exner created Chrysler's "Flight Sweep Styling" suite, with the 300C as its centerpiece.

The 300C's standard Hemi engine produced 375 horsepower. The low hood line required an inventive air cleaner design for the dual quad carburetors.

Chrysler put plenty of grunt beneath the hood, as a properly optioned 300C could boast of having 375 horsepower to help it rocket down the road. Sales for the high-profile vehicle were good, as 2,251 units went to good homes.

(above) The 1957 Chrysler was one of the first cars to integrate the front bumper into the overall design of the car's front end. The 1957 Chrysler was also one the first cars to use quad headlights.

While the 300C couldn't quite bury the impressive speedometer, it could propel the flagship Chrysler well into triple-digit territory.

(above) Beneath the headlights were functional brake cooling ducts, much needed on a hefty car with drum brakes and the horsepower to blur the scenery.

When it came to developing staggering amounts of power on the street, few could rival the 375-horsepower Hemi, complete with dual four-barrel carburetors.

Even with the AMA ban on racing in effect, buyers snapped up the brutally fast 300C. Chrysler matched the new exterior styling and increased power with improved ride and a more stable chassis. The 300C owner's manual even advised buyers to handle its power with care.

(above) With a Hemi under the hood, full instrumentation helped to keep the engine healthy.

Huge tail fins were a handy place to mount the 300C's identification medallion.

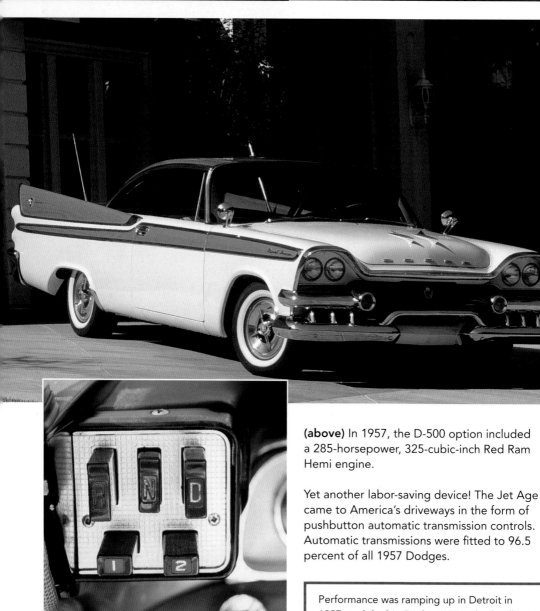

(above) In 1957, the D-500 option included a 285-horsepower, 325-cubic-inch Red Ram Hemi engine.

Yet another labor-saving device! The Jet Age came to America's driveways in the form of pushbutton automatic transmission controls. Automatic transmissions were fitted to 96.5 percent of all 1957 Dodges.

Performance was ramping up in Detroit in 1957, and the big Dodge (118-inch wheelbase) could be equipped with the optional ground-pounding Super D-500 Hemi churning out an impressive 310 horsepower.

Subtle wasn't a term that could be applied to most 1950s-era vehicles, and the 1957 Dodge did its part to uphold the visual drama that Detroit embraced.

Snazzy oval exhaust tips worked with the fighter jet–inspired styling, most noteworthy being the "rocket exhaust" taillights trimmed in chrome and the massive two-tone fins.

(above) Though it was based on the New Yorker, the 300C was significantly different, from its Virgil Exner styling to its beefy Hemi V-8 engine.

Built using body-on-frame construction, the 300C surprised many with its excellent road manners, thanks to its torsion bar front suspension and the advanced rear leaf spring suspension. At the Daytona racetrack, a 300C passed through the Flying Mile at 134 mph.

Displacing 392 cubic inches, the Hemi-head engine delivered up to 390 horsepower, depending on options.

No manufacturer did fins like Chrysler. Called "rear stabilizers" by Chrysler, it was claimed that they improved high-speed stability.

Taking the entire family anywhere was a non-issue with a 300C. A fold-down arm rest was provided for the front seat occupants.

(above) With its heavily lidded headlights and long, dramatic tail fins, the Coronet was a strong presence on the road.

Displacing 326 cubic inches, the Red Ram engine generated 255 horsepower at 4,400 rpm. It had 9.2:1 compression and utilized a Carter two-barrel carburetor.

The Dodge Coronet Custom Royal tipped the scales at 3,675 pounds. Buyers wanting maximum performance could spring for the Super D-500 engine option, displacing 383 cubic inches and generating 345 horsepower.

(above) From the rear, the Coronet resembled a jet fighter, exactly the impression the designers wanted. The tall fins aided in backing maneuvers.

The exterior wasn't the only area that boasted "modern" styling. The interior had more than a little Space Age flavor to it.

Sports Cars

Following World War II, young American soldiers returned from Europe and talked about the sporty, smaller cars being driven there. The two-seat MG, while not over-powered, was a fun car to drive and one that would turn heads as it went down the street. The 1950s-era Crosleys were small and interesting cars, but they had little sex appeal. In 1954, Kaiser released its attractive fiberglass Kaiser-Darrin sports car, but a hefty price tag ensured its demise. Chrysler also teamed up with Italy's premier design studio, Ghia, to produce a striking and powerful but short-lived 1950s sports car—the Dual Ghia. The 1950–1954 Muntz Jet was another attempt at building a unique, sporty car, but it just about drove its creator, Earl "Mad Man" Muntz, to the poorhouse. The 1953 Nash-Healy was another attempt by a small niche automaker to build a sports car, but its high cost was its downfall as well. It would take dedication and deep pockets to fund a sports car program in the 1950s, and only two automakers fit that description: Chevrolet and Ford.

Chevrolet Corvette

Chevrolet introduced its Corvette sports car in 1953 and touted it as the first of the Motorama dream cars to be produced. Their ads stated, "It packs more sheer fun into every mile than any other car you've ever driven."

Previous spread: 1954 Chevrolet Corvette

Under the sleek new fiberglass body, Chevrolet fitted a scaled-down passenger car frame and a six-cylinder engine backed by a Powerglide automatic. Chevrolet's engineering staff modified the engine for more power and added three side-draft carburetors that provided more power and a lower hood line.

Chevrolet produced only 300 Corvettes that first year, and anxious buyers snapped them all up. In anticipation of huge sales, Chevrolet upped production of the Corvette for 1954 to 3,640 units. But the bright shine on the new Corvette's fenders wore off quickly, and many sat unsold for months. Thankfully, Ford came to the rescue by announcing that it would be producing its own sports car in 1955, the Thunderbird. Not to be outdone, Chevrolet would continue the Corvette and even redesign it for 1956. It was shaping up to be a battle of the Titans, with the consumer as the ultimate winner.

With the battle for the American sports car title on the line, Chevrolet completely redesigned its 1956 Corvette and added plenty of power. Zora Arkus-Duntov, who had joined Chevrolet's engineering team, saw the potential in Chevrolet's new V-8 and added two four-barrel carburetors and a long-duration cam to increase the 265 engine's horsepower to 225. This, along with the stunning new body and interior, resulted in a successful sales year in 1956, with 3,467 units sold. The number may not seem high by today's standards, but it was a giant leap over the previous year's sales of only 700 units.

Chevrolet's engineering team worked long and hard to develop its fuel-injection unit for 1957 that increased displacement to 283 and boosted horsepower to 283 as well. One horsepower per cubic inch had been a benchmark of performance that engineers had dreamed about for years, and Chevrolet was the first to offer such an engine in its Corvette sports car. Chevrolet also made that horsepower more user-friendly with the addition of a four-speed manual transmission and a Posi-Traction rear axle.

For 1958, Chevrolet's designers gave the Corvette a new body, featuring attractive side coves, quad headlights, and sexy curves. It also had an excess of design elements, such as rows of fake hood louvers and long chrome moldings that ran down the deck lid. Chevrolet's engineers also bumped up the horsepower on the top-rate fuel-injected engine to 290 horsepower. They made improvements to the chassis, giving serious racers the ability to successfully compete in professional-level races. The Corvette's appeal continued to grow throughout the decade, with sales of the 1959 model totaling 9,670 units.

Ford Thunderbird

Ford's product planners also saw that sports cars were becoming exceptionally popular in the early 1950s. The release of the 1953 Chevrolet Corvette must have sent the Ford executives in Dearborn scrambling. Ford had considered a sports car earlier, but the 0.27 percent of the total U.S. market taken by sports cars brought them back to reality. But the 1953 Corvette changed the game, and Ford engineers began to work on their own sports car, named Thunderbird in honor of the Native Americans' god of prosperity and rain.

Ford unveiled its first Thunderbird concept car at the 1954 Detroit Auto Show. Although only a wooden mockup, it gave the Ford faithful something to look forward to. When Ford's 1955 Thunderbird hit the market, the only resemblance between it and the Corvette was the 102-inch wheelbase. Ford's design and engineering staff had created a stylish car that looked like a member of the Ford family of cars and offered a much better engineered steel body than the Corvette's fiberglass body. It featured a powerful 292-cubic-inch V-8 engine. Ford geared up for higher production levels and outsold Corvette at a rate of almost 24 to 1 with 16,155 units moving off dealer lots at the end of 1955. The guys in Dearborn must have been giddy with those numbers, especially since they had come to the sports car market two years late.

Ford made only a few cosmetic changes to the 1956 Thunderbird. Engineers increased the horsepower of the base 292-cubic-inch engine and offered an optional 312-cubic-inch engine. Bill Boyer, the original designer, suggested adding optional portholes to the hardtop. The buyers loved this no-cost option, and it soon became part of the Thunderbird's iconic look. Sales of 1956 Thunderbirds slacked off slightly to 15,631 units, still outpacing the Corvette at a rate of five to one.

Ford's design staff did a wonderful job of redesigning the 1957 Thunderbird. The Ford engine group also stepped up to the plate and added more horsepower, including a supercharged version of its 312-cubic-inch engine. Still priced under $3,500, slightly higher than the Corvette, it did well, selling a record 21,380 units.

With Ford riding high on the sales of its 1957 Thunderbird, marketers deviated from the traditional path of playing it safe by discontinuing the two-seat version in favor of an all new four-seat Thunderbird for 1958. Ford's market research found a huge untapped segment of the population that wanted an upscale, sporty car that could seat four passengers. So Ford banked on the Thunderbird nameplate and created a personal luxury car for 1958. The gamble paid off, and Ford was able to sell 38,000 of the new T-Birds. Ford would command this segment of the market until Buick released its Riviera in 1963. Smart marketing added to the bottom line but ended the short run of one of the most attractive American sports cars ever built.

Today, we take two-seat sports cars for granted. Almost every manufacturer has at least one in the market. But in the 1950s, auto manufacturers thought the American car-buying public would buy them up more readily. Surprisingly, and thankfully, Chevrolet continued with its Corvette through the 1950s. Its survival depended on strong sales of Chevrolet's passenger cars and an upper management team that enjoyed high-performance image cars.

Only about 15 percent of the model year production was painted Pennant Blue. Wire mesh headlight covers suggested the European sports cars that used a similar treatment to protect the expensive lenses.

Only one engine was available in the 1954 Corvette, the rugged "Stovebolt Six," an inline six-cylinder engine displacing 235.5 cubic inches and rated at 150 horsepower.

It's generally acknowledged that the 1955 Thunderbird saved the Corvette from extinction. Sales of the Chevy sports car were soft. Yet, when Ford's personal car debuted and its sales took off, GM decided to fight back, launching the Corvette on the performance path it travels to this day.

In order to open the door from the outside, one had to reach in to actuate the interior handle. As the 1954 Corvette lacked rigid, roll-up side windows, it was not a problem.

Long, tapered taillight housings were graceful stylistic elements allowed by the use of fiberglass as the body material.

With its sleek European-inspired lines and "rocket" tail lights, the 1954 Corvette caught the imagination. Exhaust fumes tended to swirl around the back of the car, filling the cabin with exhaust.

Chevrolet had hoped to sell 10,000 Corvettes in 1954, but the public was less than willing to spend $2,774 on a car that didn't even have door locks. Only 3,640 were built, and the Corvette's future seemed doomed. But Zora Arkus-Duntov convinced Chevrolet's management to put some real power under the hood and improve the handling. The result was a world-class sports car, then and now.

Only one engine was available in the 1954 Corvette: the trusty Stovebolt Six. Rated at 155-horsepower, it could get the Corvette up to 60 mph in just 11 seconds.

Unlike many vehicles from Detroit in 1954, the Corvette used a minimum of chrome. The wire mesh over the headlights was a nod to European sports cars.

Unlike most sports cars of the day, the Corvette was relatively luxurious. To open the door, you had to reach inside to pull the release.

With a serial number of #005, this was the first production Thunderbird built. It was used in a 1954 *Sports Illustrated* road test before being sold to the public.

Displacing 292 cubic inches, the V-8 in the 1955 Thunderbird was rated at 193 horsepower when bolted to a manual gearbox, 198 horses when attached to an automatic transmission.

Ford barely beat General Motors to the trademark office to register the "Thunderbird" name. GM wanted to use the name on a concept vehicle. They had to resort to choice number two: Firebird. Ford used the opulence of the Thunderbird to draw potential buyers into the showroom to view the entire Ford line.

The exhaust tips exited from chromed housings in the 1955 model, but starting in 1956, the tips were located at the ends of the rear bumper.

Ford fitted its upscale 1955 Thunderbird with a classy mixture of high-quality vinyl upholstery, deep pile carpet, and attention to build quality.

Essentially a race car disguised as a 1956 Thunderbird, the 15 D/F cars started life as "D" code cars, then fitted with the supercharged "F" code engine package.

With a belt-driven McCullough/Paxton VR57 centrifugal air pump bolted on, the "F" engine developed 340 horsepower.

Due to the high-velocity airflow that the supercharger pumped out, Ford replaced the standard Holley four-barrel carburetor with a modified Lincoln version of the high-rise Holley.

For a 1955 Thunderbird, the D/F cars were stripped. With a floor-mounted shifter and no radio, it wasn't the ideal car for date night.

Attached to a stout four-speed manual transmission, the D/F cars couldn't use an automatic transmission because of the slushbox's inability to handle the power.

Visually a carryover model from 1956, the '57 Corvette started injecting serious power under the hood, including the new-for-'57 fuel injection.

The vast majority of Corvette buyers in 1957 in search of serious performance equipped their new purchases with the optional dual-quad carburetors. It generated two levels of power, 245 and 270 horsepower, the difference being due to a special camshaft in the higher-rated engine.

This was the last year for the single-headlight body style on the solid axle platform. This was the first year that the Corvette could boast of having one horsepower per cubic inch, in this case 283.

Chevrolet adopted a clean, symmetrical layout for the dashboard. Though reading the gauges could be a challenge, especially at night, the design was handsome.

Recessed taillights helped to give the '57 a clean profile.

The Thunderbird was available in a full palate of striking colors, including Coral Sand and Raven Black.

Ford was serious about injecting performance into the Thunderbird in 1957 to combat the increasingly powerful Corvette. Buyers of the E-Series engine enjoyed a 285-horsepower, 312-cubic-inch V-8 that utilized stiffer valve springs, an aggressive camshaft, and 10.0:1 compression when fitted with the Racing Kit. Total Thunderbird production for 1957 was 21,380 units.

Twin raised domes covered the two Holley 4000 carburetors. Chrome and cast aluminum helped dress up the engine compartment.

The turquoise inset on the Thunderbird referenced the Southwestern source of the Thunderbird legend.

Ford added the circular taillight and fin to maintain the visual continuity across the 1957 Ford lineup.

Like a strong fist wrapped in velvet, the Phase II Thunderbirds were rarely seen, as only 194 were built in 1957.

Using lessons learned from the potent D/F Thunderbirds, the Phase II cars used a revised McCullough/Paxton VR57A blower developed for full-sized Fords and the Thunderbird.

With its air plenum peeking above the fender, the 300-horsepower, supercharged V-8 could spank almost any vehicle it chose.

154

Ford hit the personal car target dead center with the Thunderbird, creating an inviting interior that begged for long drives on summer nights.

Hooded headlights were a stylistic element that Ford employed across most of the lineup, establishing a familial look.

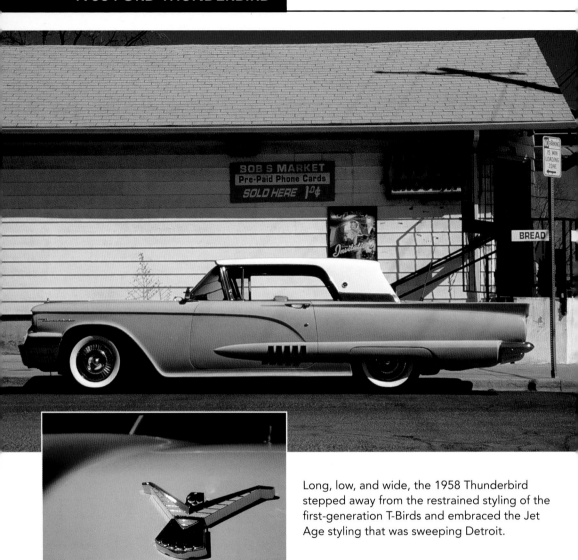

Long, low, and wide, the 1958 Thunderbird stepped away from the restrained styling of the first-generation T-Birds and embraced the Jet Age styling that was sweeping Detroit.

Ford freshened the Thunderbird's nose emblem in 1958, creating a "V" with the wings to denote a V-8 engine beneath the front-hinged hood.

Ford introduced a four-seat Thunderbird in 1958, essentially handing the two-seat sports car market to the Corvette. Yet with model year sales of 37,892 units compared to the Corvette's 9,168, Ford executives were popping champagne corks.

Looking just as much at home on the flight line as the driveway, the 1958 Thunderbird employed such styling elements as vents, spears, and arcing lines to evoke a sense of power and speed.

The Thunderbird stylists fitted a back-up light to the center of the taillights. The mesh design on the area surrounding the taillights matched the grille material.

Scaglietti's three coupes had nearly identical lines. He fitted each car with Borrani wire wheels. To make clear the car's lineage, he installed the "chrome teeth" grille into each car, though over time at least one of the owners removed the Corvette grille.

Three enthusiasts—Texas oilman and Chevrolet dealer Gary Laughlin, and racers Carroll Shelby and Jim Hall—approached Sergio Scaglietti to build something special for them. Scaglietti produced three nearly identical coupes, one for each of them. However, the costs of shutting down the St. Louis Corvette line to build three body-less cars cost too much, dooming the project's future. Shelby took the idea of an American engine in a European body to Ford, and the Cobra was born.

It's no accident that the coupes resemble period Ferrari's, as Scaglietti was one of the design firms that bodied the Maranello-based firm's chassis.

Scaglietti provided leather-covered racing seats in the otherwise simple interior.

Beneath the curvaceous Italian bodywork was a 1959 Corvette, including a 290-horsepower, fuel-injected, 283-cubic-inch V-8. Two of the cars used a four-speed manual, the third employed an automatic transmission.

Two-tone paint schemes were popular in 1959, but Indian Turquoise over Colonial White was somewhat unusual.

Dramatic brows over the headlights did little for aerodynamics, but from a visual drama stand-point, they continued the look started in 1955.

Two engines were available in the 1959 Thunderbird: the standard 352 Thunderbird Special and the optional 430-cubic-inch Thunderbird Special, fitted with a four-barrel carb, 10.0:1 compression, and rated at 350 horsepower. Buyers of this engine could only get the Cruise-O-Matic transmission.

As the four-seat Thunderbird entered its second year of production, sales took off, with a total of 67,456 units sold.

Each front fender wore a Thunderbird emblem at the front of a chrome spear. Hinting at gun sights from fighter aircraft, this stylistic element found its way onto many '50s-era automobiles.

Orphan Cars

Orphan Cars

Throughout the decade of the 1950s, the Big Three automakers (Ford, General Motors, and Chrysler) had a lock on the U.S. automotive market. All had expanded over years and had maintained their strength by producing a wide variety of vehicles. But several small automakers were still hanging on by their fingernails. They produced some unique and usually smaller vehicles than the Big Three. By the end of the 1950s, most of these companies would no longer be in business, having been swallowed up by the Big Three. But each made an impact on the market in its own distinctive way, leaving behind a legacy of special cars that will never be forgotten.

Manufacturers of these special cars (often referred to as "orphan cars") had done well when they had were on a more even footing with the Big Three in the 1930s. Many of them prospered throughout the war by providing goods and services to the government. Following the war, they were not able to recover as quickly. Most of these manufacturers also built smaller, more fuel-efficient cars that were not sought after by the buying public, since gasoline was only 19 cents per gallon.

Previous spread: 1950 Studebaker Champion

Crosley

In 1939, Powell Crosley Jr., an American industrialist who made his money in radios and refrigerators, decided to build a small car. His car sold for a maximum price of $350, could run at 50 miles per hour, and got 50 miles to the gallon. Naturally, he sold it through his network of Crosley appliance stores. Until production ceased during the war in 1942, he sold just over 7,000 cars. Production resumed in 1946, and sales volume increased every year with a peak production of 29,000 in 1948; but sales fell off for 1949. In 1950, Crosleys were built as sedans, station wagons, and two sports car–like roadsters: the Hot Shot and the Super Sport. Crosley offered disc brakes in 1950, but corrosion problems caused so many warranty headaches that they were quickly discontinued for 1951. Sales continued to fall, with only 2,075 cars sold in 1952. In July of that year, Powell Crosley sold the company to the General Tire and Rubber Company, which quickly disposed of the assets, closing forever the Crosley car company.

Henry J/Allstate/Kaiser-Frazer

The Henry J, Allstate, Kaiser, and Frazer cars of the 1950s all share a short but complex history. Joseph Frazer was a Washington blue-blood aristocrat who loved cars. From the 1920s through the 1940s, he worked for Packard, Pierce-Arrow, and General Motors. Following the war, Frazer teamed up with Henry J. Kaiser, who had made a fortune during the war by producing Liberty ships. In 1945, they formed the Kaiser-Frazer Corporation and moved their production headquarters into a former bomber plant at Willow Run, Michigan. They hired body designer Howard Darrin to design the mid-level Kaiser and the upscale Frazer. But selling an upscale car in the early 1950s without a V-8 engine was an almost impossible task. The last of the Frazers rolled off the assembly line in 1951.

Kaisers continued to sell well through the early 1950s, especially after Darrin's redesigned models hit the market in 1951. They called the new look the "Anatomic Design." It featured a lower beltline and more glass than any other car coming out of Detroit. It also included safety features, such as a padded instrument panel, slender roof pillars for greater visibility, and recessed instruments. In an attempt to get some positive press in 1954, a sports car built on a design that Darrin created in 1952 was released. The Kaiser-Darrin featured a fiber-glass body and sliding passenger doors. They were built on a 100-inch Henry J chassis. Only 435 were built before production ended. Designer Darrin bought the remaining units (fewer than 100), installed a Cadillac V-8, and sold them in a Los Angeles showroom for $4,350 each. In 1954, production of all Kaiser vehicles ended.

In 1950, in addition to the high-end Frazer and mid-level Kaiser, Kaiser-Frazer created a short-wheelbase compact car derived from its 1951 Kaiser. The Henry J, a little fastback sedan with modest tail fins, was named the "Fashion Car of the Year" in 1951 by the New York Fashion Academy. Power came from either a 68-horsepower, four-cylinder engine or an 80-horsepower, six-cylinder engine. The 1951 models sold well, but sales declined until production ceased in 1954. The Henry J was renamed "Allstate" and was sold by Sears, Roebuck, and Company in 1952 and 1953.

Hudson

The Hudson motorcar had a 49-year run that ended in 1957. The Hudsons of the late 1940s were stylish and very well built cars. In 1948, Hudson introduced its "step-down" design, producing a sleek car with a low center of gravity. In the early 1950s, the Hudsons were the darlings of the NASCAR circuit because of their excellent handling and strong aerodynamic bodies. But Hudson could not meet the changes that were occurring within the auto industry in the mid-1950s. On January 1, 1954, Hudson merged with Nash-Kelvinator, forming American Motors. But the move was more of a take-over of Hudson than a merger, and many Hudson models were cut. The 1955 Hudsons were merely Nashes with different trim. A V-8 engine would be added in 1955, but it would not be enough to save the Hudson nameplate, which was discontinued after the 1957 model year.

Studebaker

As 1950 dawned, Studebaker executives blew out the 98 candles on the corporate cake celebrating it as America's most senior maker of wheeled vehicles. It was also one of Studebaker's best production years, with 329,884 units sold. Studebakers featured the creations of legendary industrial designer Raymond Loewy. The Studebaker Commanders of the early 1950s featured a sleek, pointed nose that resembled the front of a fighter aircraft. Studebaker called it the "Next Look," but no other automakers copied it, and the look quickly fell out of fashion with the American car-buying public. The attractive Champion Deluxe coupe featured excellent styling, but it was most likely ahead of its time. Studebaker struggled through most of the 1950s with cars that were overpriced. In 1954, Packard bought Studebaker. The brightest spot for Studebaker in the late 1950s had to have been the 1959 introduction of its compact Lark, just as the buying public was moving toward compact cars. But this joy was short lived as the company went into free fall and eventually closed its doors in 1959.

Nash/Rambler

Following the war, Nash did quite well with its Airflyte design. It was a step ahead of all other carmakers and offered features like a one-piece curved windshield and optional seat belts, years ahead of the Big Three. In 1950, the company introduced the Rambler, a much smaller car than the Nash. They hoped that the buying public would be drawn to the Rambler because the Big Three had nothing of its size available. The Rambler sold well because the market was ready for anything new. In 1952, Nash and Healy, a British sports car manufacturer, joined forces to create the Nash-Healy roadster. It featured an all-aluminum body designed by Pinin Farina and was powered by a Nash 125-horsepower, six-cylinder engine. The high cost of manufacturing the car and shipping the bodies from England to the United States was its downfall. Production ended in 1953.

Nash, however, did not completely abandon the idea of a small, two-seat car with the demise of its Nash-Healy. In January 1954, Nash introduced the tiny 85-inch-wheelbase, Metropolitan. Its 42-horsepower, 74-cubic-inch engine could squeeze 40 miles from a gallon of gas. These miniscule cars came in two models, a hardtop and a convertible, each priced at less than $1,500. In 1954, Nash acquired Hudson and formed American Motors. In 1955, the Hudson cars were just Nashes with Hudson markings. But while the Big Three were moving cars as fast as beer at a July baseball game, the Nash/Hudson/Rambler cars were taking root in dealers' lots. The last Nash cars would be sold in 1957, with the Rambler nameplate continuing on. But as the decade came to a close, America's taste for small cars improved, and the Rambler sold well.

Willys

The name Willys is usually associated with World War II Jeeps. But in 1928 Willys was third in production behind Chevrolet and Ford. In 1950, Willys capitalized on the Jeep's popularity with the release of its Jeepster. The Jeepster phaeton convertible had the classic cues of the World War II Jeep in a more family-friendly package. The optimistic feeling of the early 1950s led Willys to move back into the passenger car arena. In 1952, they released the Aero-Wing sedan. Sales suffered because of the high price of the car. In 1954, Henry Kaiser bought out Willys and combined it with his Kaiser-Frazer Company. But in 1955, with only 5,905 models completed, the Willys car line was discontinued. It simply could not compete in the same arena as Ford or Chevrolet.

Packard

In the 1930s and 1940s, Packard motorcars were among the finest automobiles in America, rivaled only by Cadillac and Lincoln. During the war years, the company built engines for P-51 Mustangs and PT boats. The experience gained by designing and building these overhead engines led to powerful automotive V-8 engines in the 1950s. Packard engineering and quality had always been a trademark of the brand. But in 1952, the demand for Packards fell off sharply. For the 1953 model year, Packard released the Caribbean, designed by Richard Teague. The Caribbean featured a well-integrated continental kit and chrome wire wheels. It listed at well over $5,000 and had the same appeal as Cadillac's new Eldorado. In 1954, Packard and Studebaker merged. But two companies in freefall did not create a stronger company. The last real Packards were produced in 1956, and after that they were just re-badged Studebakers. In 1958, Packard ended its production forever, taking with it the Studebaker name.

In the 1950s, the automotive landscape was dotted with a variety of interesting cars and carmakers that all tried to give the customer something different in terms of style and content. But the economies of scale enjoyed by the Big Three were a tremendous advantage. Eventually, all of these smaller companies were either squeezed out of the market or forced to join together in order to survive.

1953 Nash Healey

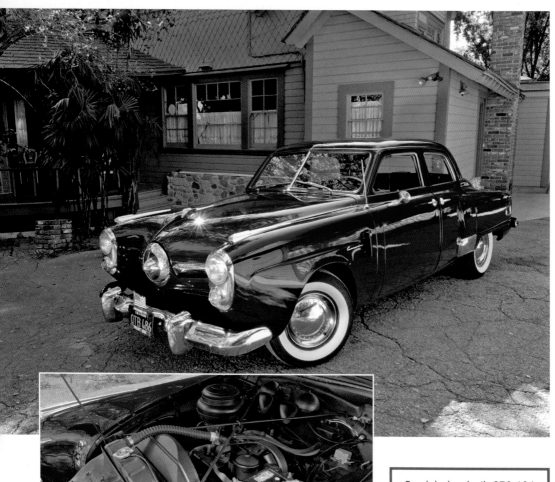

(top) Promoted as a "New Look," the Studebaker wore new front and rear sheet metal in an attempt to freshen the line.

(inset) In the Champion, an inline six-cylinder engine utilizing an L-head valve configuration displaced 169.9 cubic inches and generated 85 horsepower.

Studebaker built 270,604 Champion models in 1950 as America recovered from World War II and wanted fresh, new designs in their cars. The "Bullet Nose" design was new for 1950. Studebaker was America's ninth biggest carmaker for 1950.

(top) Studebaker positioned the seats between the axles for a lower center of gravity while promoting it as having a "Cradled Ride."

(inset) The impressive hood ornament served as a convenient handle when raising and lowering the heavy hood.

(top) Exhibiting bathtub-like lines, the 1951 Nash Rambler Convertible Sedan attracted owners that Nash assured us would fill the Social Directory or Who's Who.

(bottom) By folding the roof back, occupants could work on their suntans while the vehicle maintained structural integrity with full-frame doors.

This model of Nash Rambler may look familiar to baby-boomers who watched a lot of television in the 1950s. We would often see it stopping in front of the Daily Planet, where Lois Lane would let out Clark Kent and Jimmy Olsen after tracking down a breaking news story.

Nash owners tended to shy away from the ostentatious, and the 1951 Rambler stayed true to their desires, as evidenced by the Spartan interior.

Displacing 172.6 cubic inches, the straight six-cylinder engine in the 1951 Nash Rambler was rated at 82 horsepower.

It's thought that less than 600 FarmOroad's were built in its three-year production run.

Built from 1950 through 1952, the Crosley FarmOroad was designed to be comfortable both in a rural environment and in the city.

The dealer announcement in 1950 really says it all: "Here at last is the machine people have been wishing for and longing for—as a tractor, a powerful work horse for farming, plowing, cultivation, mowing, and so forth—a fast economical vehicle for road trips—a rugged truck of towing and hauling—a mobile power plant for sawing wood, spraying, etc, all combined in one lightweight, low-cost machine. That is the Crosley FarmOroad." And only $795! Who wouldn't want one?

Two spring clips under the outside back of the body would release the cargo box. A power take-off is visible, designed to operate a wide range of farming implements.

Like everything on the FarmOroad, the interior was minimal. Owners wanting a right-side windshield wiper paid extra.

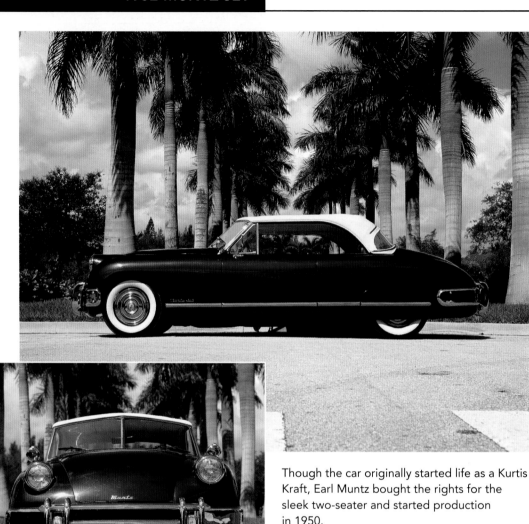

Though the car originally started life as a Kurtis Kraft, Earl Muntz bought the rights for the sleek two-seater and started production in 1950.

During the four-year production run, Muntz claimed to have lost close to half a million dollars due to the high cost of building each car. Most were virtually custom-built, with options ranging from a bar to a telephone. The Jet was a quick car, capable of reaching 60 mph in 6.7 seconds and exhibiting a top speed of 119 mph.

Muntz himself said that labor costs of each Jet were $2,000, but the publicity the car garnered helped him sell more used cars, his core business.

Stamped-steel wheel covers featured the logo of "Mad Man" Muntz.

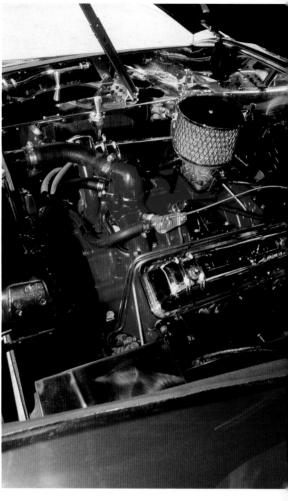

Muntz used a Lincoln flathead V-8 once production shifted from Gardena, California, to Evanston, Illinois.

With its sleek lines and low center of gravity, the Hudson Hornet was a race winner in NASCAR in the early 1950s.

Well-built and sturdy, the Hornet excelled at NASCAR's early tracks, almost exclusively dirt tracks, at a time when stock car racing actually used stock cars. The 308 engine made gobs of torque at low rpm, allowing drivers to barrel through the competition. Between 1951 and 1955, the Hudson Hornet won more than 80 races. *Photos by Mike Mueller*

(top left) The roomy Hornet could hold six adults with ease while giving a race driver plenty of elbow room.

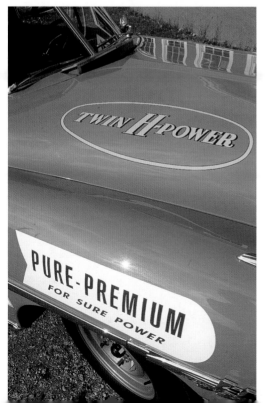

(top right) Twin H-Power was Hudson's answer to demands for power. The big 308-cubic-inch, straight six-cylinder cranked out 165 horsepower.

(left) Hudson dealers made "Severe Usage" parts available to customers to install on their Hornets for competition use.

Using Cadillac mechanicals, Italian coach-builder Ghia constructed two "concept" cars.

At one time owned and driven by actress Rita Hayworth, this car was featured on the cover of *Road & Track* magazine.

The enormous rear window eliminated any blind spots and gave the greenhouse a flowing look.

With a short front overhang and a long rear overhang, the stance of the 1953 Cadillac Ghia exuded speed.

Ghia retained an "egg-crate" grille, used by Cadillac for decades. Speed lines down the side of the vehicle visually broke up the vast expanse of sheet metal.

The Dragon was a very well-equipped sedan that was introduced on Halloween Day, 1952. Only 1,277 were sold in 1953.

Though the Dragon name had been used in 1951 as a trim option to the Deluxe model, the 1953 Dragon was a stand-alone, top-shelf vehicle. In 1953, $3,924 was a lot of money, and the Dragon was a lot of car. Kaiser pulled out all the stops and created a car that could go toe-to-toe with Cadillac. *Photos by Mike Mueller*

The richly appointed interior was loaded with comfort features, including air conditioning, heater, door lock shields, and windshield washers.

It was no problem for three adults to fit comfortably in the rear seat of the Kaiser Dragon. The fold-down center armrest was a class touch. Note the "Bambu" vinyl upholstery.

Designed by Italian designer Pinin Farina, the Nash Healey was a brisk two-seater weighing 2,400 pounds.

As befitting an American car with sporting pretensions, the Nash Healey wore wire wheel hubcaps emblazoned with the Nash emblem.

A true international effort, the American running gear and chassis were shipped to England, where the suspension was affixed. Then the chassis was sent to Turin, Italy, where Pinin Farina attached the hand-built bodies. In the 1950s TV series *Superman*, Clark Kent (George Reeves) drove a silver 1953 Nash Healey. *Photos by Mike Mueller*

Under the hood lived a "Le Mans" Dual Jetfire 234.8-cubic-inch, straight six-cylinder engine. With 8.0:1 compression, it was rated at 125 horsepower.

As an essentially European sports car, the Nash Healey's interior used large circular gauges and a "banjo"-style steering wheel.

Shipping magnate Henry J. Kaiser intended the Henry J to be an affordable economy car. It was built at Willow Run, Michigan.

Kaiser used as few parts as possible to keep costs down. Items like glove boxes, passenger-side sun visors, and arm rests cost extra. Americans did not appreciate paying extra for items they felt should be standard, and the resulting loss of sales caused the Henry J to cease production in 1954. *Photos by Mike Mueller*

The plastic hood ornament was designed to resemble a rocket in flight, a fanciful bit of hope for the budget car.

A classy design touch was the vehicle logo in chrome mounted on the driver's side of the hood.

The Henry J wore its name in handsome script at the rear of the vehicle above the license plate.

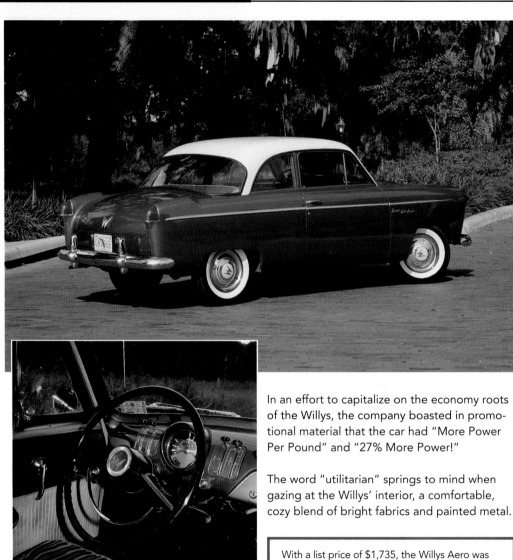

In an effort to capitalize on the economy roots of the Willys, the company boasted in promotional material that the car had "More Power Per Pound" and "27% More Power!"

The word "utilitarian" springs to mind when gazing at the Willys' interior, a comfortable, cozy blend of bright fabrics and painted metal.

With a list price of $1,735, the Willys Aero was targeting the vast majority of potential buyers at the close of the Korean War. Unfortunately, most American buyers wanted a car with more pizzazz, flash, and power. The resulting lack of sales in 1954, 1,380, didn't do much for Willys' coffers. The following year, 1955, was the last year of production for Willys. *Photos by Mike Mueller*

Trim lines and compact dimensions spoke of the modest intent of the Willys.

With economy at its core, the Willys didn't wear a lot of flashy chrome or expensive sheet metal. Instead, sturdy bumpers and clean, simple taillights graced the vehicle.

When you talk rare, the one-year-only production of the President Speedster ranks near the head of the list. This model was the top-shelf Studebaker, starting at $3,253.

Studebaker was suffering from soft sales in 1953 and 1954, so it felt that a halo vehicle would call attention to the company's offerings. Loaded to the gills with desirable comfort items, such as tinted glass, an eight-tube radio, and two-speed wipers, the Speedster packed a lot of car for the money. Unfortunately for Studebaker, only 2,215 were sold.

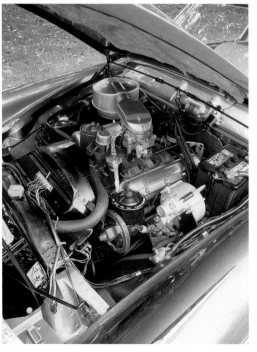

(top left) As a vehicle with sport leanings, the instrument panel was full of easy-to-read gauges.

(top right) As a premium vehicle, the interior was swathed in premium materials.

(left) The heart of the beast was a 259-cubic-inch V-8 that generated 185-horsepower and 258 lb-ft of torque.

Only 117 Dual Ghias were built, and many of them were purchased by Hollywood's rich and famous.

The A-list of 1950s Dual Ghia owners included popular Hollywood celebrities like Debbie Reynolds, Lucille Ball, and Frank Sinatra. Each owned one of these cars at one time or another, and so did a few of Sinatra's pals in the famous "Rat Pack." Rat-Packer Peter Lawford even drove one on his television series, *The Thin Man*.

While Italian coachbuilder Ghia constructed the curvaceous body, the drivetrain was pure Chrysler in the form of the D-500, 315-cubic-inch Hemi.

It took in excess of $7,600 to put a Dual Ghia in the garage. The conservative styling belied superb workmanship.

Large, easy-to-read gauges drew upon the European influence of Ghia. Machine-turned surround lent a sporty look.